T0208788

POETICALLY SPEAKING
KAREN'S RAYS

OF
THOUGHTS AND OBSERVATIONS
ON LIFE

A COUPLE SONGS OUR RETIREMENT TRIP
AND SOME OTHER SUBJECTS

KAREN (TAYLOR) RITZER

ARCHWAY
PUBLISHING

Archway Publishing books may be ordered through booksellers or by contacting:

Archway Publishing
1663 Liberty Drive
Bloomington, IN 47403
www.archwaypublishing.com
844-669-3957

Because of the dynamic nature of the Internet, any web addresses or
links contained in this book may have changed since publication and
may no longer be valid. The views expressed in this work are solely those
of the author and do not necessarily reflect the views of the publisher,
and the publisher hereby disclaims any responsibility for them.

Any people depicted in stock imagery provided by Getty Images are
models, and such images are being used for illustrative purposes only.
Certain stock imagery © Getty Images.

ISBN: 978-1-6657-3197-3 (sc)
ISBN: 978-1-6657-3196-6 (hc)
ISBN: 978-1-6657-3198-0 (e)

Library of Congress Control Number: 2022919743

Print information available on the last page.

Archway Publishing rev. date: 12/13/2022

To my children—
Rob, Tina, and Teresa—for their support and love.
Thank you.
Love you, Mom.

Contents

POEMS AND IDEAS FOR FRIENDS
AND SPECIAL OCCASIONS

SONG LYRICS

POEM FOR GRANDCHILDREN

OUR FIRST RETIREMENT TRIP

TWO POEMS ABOUT DEATH AND GRIEF AND GOING ON

MY CONDENSED BIOGRAPHY

Introduction

Some poems in this collection I wrote for this person or that cele-bration, and when we didn't have personal computers, I gave away or sent them and did not keep copies. So I don't have records of them. They have probably been thrown away long ago and not thought of again. No, I don't remember all of them.

A poem just comes to me. I write it down, sometimes hurriedly and almost unreadable. And then I type it up, and it's done. It also de-pends on what's happening in my world at the time. I write down what I get in my head and if not, it goes.........somewhere..... maybe for later, maybe not!

THOUGHTS AND OBSERVATIONS ON LIFE

Thinking of You, Tom

Walking around our abode,
How I miss you going down this road.
Thinking of things we did as us,
All the times we had things to discuss.
Talking over the daily decisions,
Wondering about car's emissions.
Listening to oldies on the car's Sirius.
Not being overly informed or curious.
Learning about politics.
Trying to teach each other, but nothing sticks.
Letting each of us have our quirks.
Side by side at work.
Bowling, fishing, cards—you name the game;
Neither of us do it at all the same.
But that was okay because, you see,
One let the other be one or "we."
There was dissension now and then,
But we always knew when to say, "We can."
The thoughts of everything
Growing closer every year,
Till the thoughts seemed as one, very clear.
My thoughts became yours and yours, mine.
Those thoughts forever became entwined.
Same as our lives became as one,
Always changing, never done.

Love became familiarity, trust, and giving
Of ourselves and in our living.
To soon, we struggled with issues of health,
Dealing with it 'cause that's what was dealt!
But it became a struggle to just stay okay,
And the days and nights just slipped away.
The struggle ended when the fight had to end.
And so goes the story of us, but on it sends.
You live on in everything here,
In our hearts and minds forever, my dear.

Anxieties

Anxiety is a funny thing.
It can tug at our heartstrings,
Pulling in all directions,
Making us think we have terrible infections,
Making us wonder what's next.
Reading about it all in text,
Studying the symptoms.
I think I have every single one.
Please keep me from thinking.
I'm reeling like I've been drinking.
Help, help make the feeling go away,
So I can function yet another day.
Put my mind to rest.
I'll try to do my best.
Those who have these thoughts
Are usually tied up in knots.
This thought process
Gives them so much stress.
Try to relax,
Access the facts,
Quit the fits,
And learn to live with it.
Calm yourself down.
Get rid of that frown.

Count backward to one,
And you're just about done.
Now put on a smile,
And after a while,
You'll no longer feel
That tug at those heartstrings.

Be the People

It's time to take a stand
Every child, woman, and man.
Make our many voices heard.
Sound the horns, spread the word.
Our beliefs in personal freedoms
And peace for all humankind.
Save the planet so it won't unwind.
Have no one country above another.
Everyone helping for a better world.
Oh, if only we all would!
Saving the planet for future generations,
One priority we all should accept.
Also being kind to each other
Would be fantastic along with respect!
Peace in all nations,
Understanding instead of hate.
We all have to try before it's too late.
Or accept our planet's death as fate.
Stand up and voice your opinion—
That's what makes this country so great!
"We the people," means you are heard;
In these United States!

(Published in *Eber and Wein*, a book of poetry.)

Because of the We in You and Me

I've seen it over and over,
How good can turn to bad.
I've seen certain circumstances change and
Make you feel so mad.

I've seen it over and over,
How it tests those who care.
It can make the best of them wonder,
Is there any help out there?

When things aren't getting better
And hardship comes to you,
There's only one thing you can do.
Square your shoulders back and say,
"You gotta do what you have to!"

When things aren't getting better,
And there is no end of it in sight,
Think of all you do have,
And things will start to work out right.

If you've got someone to share it with,
The burden will seem lighter.
Knowing you have each other
Will help things work out brighter.

Help those who love you,
And help those who don't.
For if you pass around that help,
You'll help others to care who usually won't.

Never give up the fighting
Or wanting with all your might.
For those who stick with it,
Everything will turn out right!

Don't cave in to anger, hate, or despair.
You can't help a soul if you don't care.
Last and best thing to remember
Your whole life through to do.

When all the troubles are over
And you look back to see,
You'll find they've all been conquered
Because of the you and me in *we*.

Begin Again

There comes a time in every life—
A time of indecision or of strife.

It hits us like a ton of bricks,
Leaves us feeling incomplete, sorrowed, or just sick.

Just to set these minds to rest,
Usually things will work out for the best.

Give it time and lots of thought;
Probably your fretting is for naught.

That saying, "Good things come to those who wait,"
Hogwash! We can determine our own fate!

Perseverance, hard thought, time, and good deeds
Are really all any of us needs.

Talking to someone about your woes will
Help ease the mind and really let things go.

Getting rid of dreadful thoughts and clearing the air
Set you free to let you show how much you really care.

Keep family and friends near;
They are precious, so hold them dear!

They will stick with you if you let them in,
Be by your side through thick or thin.

So hang tough, give it talk, thought, and time.
You'll be on the mend soon and feeling fine.

Mend the mind, the body, and our hearts.
Make things right again in all our parts.

In our lives, loves, families, work, or friends,
That's the way it's always been.

The beauty of this time we spend is that
Our lives can renew, and we can begin again!

Don't give up!

Children

(To mine)

Children, all ages, all kinds,
Can be so different; it blows the mind
To see how diversified they all can be,
Making, to be different, OK between you and me.
Some grow up a lot faster than others.
Some don't ever grow up, and one wonders,
What makes that difference so explicit?
How can it be? Do some have a deficit?
How can this sixteen-year-old act younger than that one?
Or one be happier and have more fun.
I guess that's where personality comes in.
Doesn't matter how they grew up or where they've been.
Don't get it wrong: upbringing means a lot.
But when it comes down to it, they have got
The wrongs and rights and how to be kind
Already embedded in their minds.
And when they grow older and go their own way,
Have families and then have to stay
Home with their own children—like it or not,
They are still children, just a whole lot.
More of them to deal with on the spot.
Because they're always your children; that *never* changes
Even though they go through the aging stages.

Love you all!

Christmas Is Coming Again

Christmas is coming again this year.
Break out the songs and feelings of cheer.
Holiday greetings as we travel about,
Searching for the right thing, in and out.
Decorations are something to see.
Most every home has put up their tree.
Lighting our homes for all to see!

People are filled with tidings of joy.
Watching out for just the right toy
For the little lad down the street
Or the little lass who wants a treat!

Families gathering for dinner, making plans.
Who will bring what? Dessert or yams?
Volunteers helping those in need.
We should all be doing good-willed deeds.

'Tis the season for all of us to take stock,
Help each other all around the block.
And throughout the whole world,
Spread His Word to be better souls
To our neighbors and friends of the fold!

May you all have the merriest Christmas of all,
And may your new year be bright,
Especially on this year's Christmas and New Year's Eve nights!

Déjà Vu

I don't know what it is or why that
Looking back makes me cry.
Can't put my finger right on it.
No specifics jump out at me or "sonics."
But memories do that to me—
Whether good, bad, or sentimental.
It seems to others I'm just mental!
Did you ever have that feeling
That sends you reeling
'Cause you know you've been there, done that?
Things happen that make you look back.
Can't quite place it or
Don't want to face it.
But you know it's very familiar.
Almost like you took a picture.
Seems so real and lifelike.
But I don't know why we fight.
To say, "Can't be! Couldn't have been!
I wasn't ever there, not now, not then!"
But the mind continues to tell you
It's familiar; it's not out of the blue.
You were there and saw it too.
Don't fight it! Just appreciate it as, déjà Vu.

(This poem was in *The Turning Corners,* published by Eber and Wein,
International Library of Poetry, and it received the Critics Choice Award.)

Depression

Too bad a poem is no cure! They say everyone has at one time or another in their lifetime experienced depression to some degree. Recognizing it and getting help for it is half the battle!

The human mind is a marvelous thing
When it's working fine and in the swing.
Things go great, and we handle stress.
When it isn't working, it can be a mess.
There is a down and darker side,
Easily misread and willing to hide.
Keeping those with such troubled minds
Unable to focus or find quieting times.
Of thoughts and processing information,
That should be a normal mind sensation.
Dark thoughts, problems, tiredness, depression
Form in the mind and leave aggression,
Or turns the person further inside, not out.
They cannot function or go about.
They feel alone and that everyone's against them.
Or simply give up and can do nothin'.
And how can we help if we do not know
What's going on with so and so?

Get the person help, and be there if needed.
Don't let the mindset systems go unheeded.
This disease cannot cure itself.
These people need care and lots of help.
To overcome and tackle this sickness
Can be done! But show no weakness!
Make them seek out professional care,
And make sure you are always there
For them to sound off and to unburden
About ailments, systems, and true feelings.
Then they, too, can have a day with normal dealings
And lead lives worthwhile and not crappy.
With normal goings on being reasonably happy.

Give a little thought and sympathy,
And all should become a reality.
That we all have our own problems and tribulations,
Teaching us to become a compilation
Of old and new thoughts and compromises,
So we can deal with all *life's surprises!*

For our friend.

Feelin's

Can't help thinkin'
Something's going to give.
Gonna hit us all
Right where we live.
Sparks will fly,
And people will get by,
But there are bound to be hard feelin's
From the sentiments that are reelin'
In their minds about each other.
Talkin' 'bout moms, dads, sisters, brothers,
All will get a twinge
When they put their two cents in.
There is always gonna be sentiments,
Hard feelin's, and resentments.
They stop the healin' process.
You have to get beyond all that.
Move forward; forget *all* the past
In order to get yourself healed.
You have to accept it and then forget it.
Deal with it and seal it!
Move on, and live to better yourself and others.
Love those moms, dads, sisters, and brothers
Unconditionally, with no fears,
Without tears, forever, through all the years.

The Fog Is So Thick:
Christmas 2019

My first thought in my head as I awoke this morning and looked out the window was, *The fog is so thick that Jolly St. Nick could not find his sleigh to make a quick getaway.* And that thought turned into this!

Santa is coming to town tonight.
Shut off your TVs and extra lights.
He does his best work when Christmas lights show his way.
And not too long at each house is he able to stay.
He knows every street and every place all around,
And he will get to each one before morning dawns.

Sometimes he arrives in a flurry of snow.
Sometimes it's raining; you never know!
And even sometimes it's really too hot,
But he still makes it to every stop!
And sometimes the fog gets so thick,
That even Jolly St. Nick
Could not see his own sleigh to make a quick getaway.

But always, Old St. Nicholas knew
All the possibilities when he flew
Could be very dangerous at night,
And he had Rudolph's red nose for light.
So he whistled and called for his sleigh,
And all the reindeer came right away,
Taking Santa off into the night.

So you see, girls and boys,
Never worry about Santa and the toys.
For he will always get through
Any obstacle that gets in his way
So you all will have a very merry Christmas Day.

Santa doesn't want you to forget those around you,
To give them a hug, and say, "Merry Christmas," to.
For family and friends are what makes
Christmastime so great to celebrate!
And so Santa says as he flies away,
"Merry Christmas to all, and have a great day!"

Merry Christmas!

For Cynthia, December 2017

There once a girl from the city.
She was so cute, witty, and pretty.
She turned sixteen and got her driver's license,
And could not wait to get on the road.
So along with her brother she drove
To the big city to get her own ride,
Driving home the Mustang with pride.
It's red and got a convertible top.
She can see in plain view all the stops.
Now she's looking for another car
So in the winter, she can drive far.
And save the Mustang for fair-weather days
And drive the other on snowy highways.
Maybe an Explorer or maybe a Jeep.
All she wants is something cheap
That will get her where she wants to go,
Through icy streets covered with snow.
Not taking too much gas from place to place
And drivable in any case.
The Jeep she chose did not like icy roads
And decided to give up.

So back to the car lots she went
So her hard-earned money could be spent
On a Mitsubishi black sedan, along with her rent.
She is graduated now and out of school,
In her own place and feeling cool.
Feeling content being on her own,
Really liking living in her space alone.
She works hard, got a job at Pure Fishing,
Till to college she goes after Thanksgiving.
Off to St. Charles in Missouri
To start learning a new career in a hurry.
Change of plans, will still start school
But in a new apartment under Spencer's rule.
So Cynthia starts a new journey at eighteen
As this year comes to an end,
And a new season of her life begins.

Love you, Cynthia, good luck. Grandma

Friends Again: Dean, 2020

From the boy I once knew
To the man he has become,
I want you to know
I love you as one!

From the knowing you then
To the knowing you when.
We would swim together at evening twilight,
But never ever did we argue or fight!

We drifted our own ways, apart.
We each kept the other
In a place in our hearts.

I look back with fondness
At our time and togetherness,
Wondering why we shouldn't find that now.
I do understand about the why and how.

So good friends we are! I can do that!
Forever hoping and wishing we could go back
To simpler times with less complications,
With fewer distractions and no obligations!

I hope our story doesn't end here,
That we will always remain near and dear.
An hour from here, or several from there,
In touch with each other always from somewhere!

Good friends we will stay
Till the end of our days!

Friends Till the End

Dean,
The years went by—sometimes slow, sometimes fast—
And we know we cannot relive the past.

The memories we'll always have,
But the future is now to travel our paths.

I hope my path is to be by your side.
My wish is that it happens, that we've tried.

I know you say, "If it is to be, it will happen."

But I'm not so sure I want to leave it to fate
For it has given us more than we needed on our plates.

You have been my rock, my adviser, my friend.
And now I want to be friends till my end.

To sit by your side as we travel the road,
Not caring which way, not being told.

Stopping whenever our hearts see a spot,
Be it desert, mountain, ocean, cold, or hot!

Time, hopefully, will become our companion,
And we can have friendship as we drive the canyons.

Making our journey through life—from the beginning
To the end—with my best friend!

Good Morning, Let the Fun Begin

Good morning,
Let the fun begin.
To start off,
Let me see you grin.

We have lots
Of work to do.
So sit down,
Take a look at a few
Things that need
Taken care of by you.

We'll start with
Our general attitude.
Good to know we can
Show a little latitude
With our fellow man.

The magic words
Should be remembered.
And we should always
Be even-tempered,
Even if it means
Keeping mouths shut.

There should never be
Any name-calling.
Always try to find
The best in everyone
To keep them from falling
Into a deep hole of despair.

Do the best you can
In everything you try to do.
Our best efforts,
Even if we do not always succeed,
Teach us a thing or two.

Winning is not always
The best thing that can happen to us.
Sometimes we learn the most
When we pick ourselves up
Out of frustrations and dust.

Hang in there!
Give it all your best shot.
Whether it be playing, education,
Job, family, love, or friendship,
You'll always be a winner
Knowing you've tried your darndest!

Growing Old ... Oh, Well

Oh, brain, oh, brain, brain, where have you gone?
It seems like forever and been so long
Since you've served me perfectly when needed. Oh, well.
I put something down, and for a while, it's gone.
I put things away, not intentionally to stay,
And hey, they're permanently lost forever! Oh, well.
Thoughts come to mind, words to put with them in kind
Escape from me time to time.
That answer back quickness has slackened.
Communication skills have become lackin'. Oh, well.
Getting up out of my chair used to be quick and easy.
Now I sit and contemplate, how unfair!
It's so far to the kitchen, way out there!
Totally all unfair and lame, but who cares? Oh, well.
I love my grandkids; they have more energy than I did.
Just watching them play and run about
Certainly is tiring and wears me out.
Can't keep up with anything like I used to. Oh, well.
Cooking, cleaning, and the laundry—can't get it all done some days.
But there's always tomorrow, right?
But tomorrow is reserved for the fight
That I have with myself for what I didn't get done. Oh, well.
I'm still living and breathing,
Still able to say, "I'm not leaving just yet."
So bring me my memories; I've at least got my senses.

They haven't stopped or been taken, not yet! Oh, well.
Until I actually do go, I'm very happy to know
It will happen for all of us, sooner for some and later for others.
I prefer to go with the, "later for others," if given my druthers. Oh, well.
I'm not going to be forcing the issue
Because if I do, I'll be deep in tissues
Thinking how old I've gotten, and wondering, *Damn, will I be forgotten
Sooner than I anticipated or ever thought?* Oh, well.
I'm going out to enjoy every minute.
That's the secret to dealing with it.
I'll stay young at heart, and that's a great start
To growing old and aging well; who can tell,
Things may go swell or go to hell, but … oh, well.

How to Get through to You

How do we get through
To the inner you?
You think everyone else
Should leave your life alone,
Let you walk your own unknown.
But people who care
Can't even dare
To think where that path will take you.

These people already know
Just how it all goes
When this path is stayed on!
Nothing but darkened despair
Can come from this line of thinking.
We've all seen it happen,
Know what comes.
Don't want this for someone we love.

So we try our darndest
And mess in your business
To show you the happier way.
But you fight every step
And think that you're kept
Away from what you want to do.
When all that we want
Is to show you what's best for you.

All our experiences
And our own mistakes,
Knowledge of this
Should count for something!
We have learned from ours
And wish to pass it along
To save others from going wrong!
It's the way it should work,
So don't be a jerk.
Take some advice from experience!

Some compromise
And thoughts of others
Should be high on a list of one's priorities.
Responsibility for one's actions
Should be what happens
In everything we say and do.
It should come to us automatically
In the form of consideration from you!

There are rules
We all have to follow.
There are deeds
We are not to allow.
There are social manners,
Interactions with fellow planners.
We all have to live together and get along,
Or our story ends up a very sad song.

In the scheme of all things,
You have to want
Good things to happen to yourself and others.
You cannot shirk
Your duty to yourself
And just not try to recover!
For what relationships of any kind
Can only rely on self-pity?

Pride, selfishness—
What good comes from that?
If you cannot share things with another,
To give of yourself and
Help others in the process.
And want what's good in you
To be discovered by another
Is ultimately what we all
Should want.

That is living!

It's Okay, Old Friend

I no longer look like the girl down the street.
I want you to know that before we meet.
The fifty-some years between then and now
Have changed me to an old woman somehow.

Maybe not so nice and a little wiser,
But worn and weathered and a lot wider!
You probably see me through eyes of long ago.
That makes me a little worried, you know!

As for you, in my heart and mind,
You're still the man who was so kind
And loving and my hero and so good to me.

I still feel that way, and I've told you so.
So don't worry on your end about this meet
Because to me, you were and now will always
Be the man I loved from up the street!

Even if that street stretched from Iowa to Minnesota
Over the years, or to South Dakota, whichever applied.

If when we do get together and meet
Some things don't work and aren't so sweet,
There will not be a problem between us
Because we will still always be friends and thus,

Old friends forever as we have been,
Friends now and forever, and then
We'll still have each other to bend
An ear or grumble to about this and that.
Friends we'll be, and I'll have your back.

So no matter how or what comes from this meet,
Our lives will be better, and that is so neat!

I'm waiting for that day with anxious anticipation, excitement,
And trepidation, and schoolgirl feelings from long ago.

It's Your Heart I See

I don't care what you look like.
It's your heart I see, and that is what is important to me!
It's not what you think, what you should do.
It's your kindness and gentleness I want too.
You're a man in my eyes because you do the right thing,
Even at a cost to your own well-being.
Others are always first for you;
That's just what you always do.
You give your soul for those you care for
And have patience and fortitude galore.
Those things and more make me care more.
I promise never again to walk away and close the door!
Even if we remain just good friends,
I'm here now for you; until our journey ends!

Kind or Bully?

I don't like you anymore, so much.
You've gotten to be a bully and such.
You push, you shove, and say nasty things.
Doing this to other people only brings
Sorrow and hurt feelings and pains.
And for what? Why? What do you gain?
People should try to be at least civil,
Instead of fighting to try to stay evil.
It makes more sense, in my mind,
To try to do good and try to be kind.
For what does it hurt to open a door,
Or give help to a stranger or even more.
The feeling you get from helping others
Is something I would rather have—
If I could have my druthers.
There has to be an end to hate.
And it cannot be just left to fate!
We have to teach our children; we have to state
That they practice and practice, do not stop or hesitate!
Or it will prove we are too late!
It has to start with each of us in our hearts and minds.
And be taught to all others: Just be kind!
That is all it should take!
Peace and kindness, wouldn't that be great!

The New Dawn

(to my children: Rob, Tina, Teresa)
It's dusk, the sun is going down
Making way for evening sights and sounds.
The birds stop chirping and lay to rest
All their little ones in the tree nest.
Crickets begin to sing their evening song
Oh, peaceful darkness all night long.
Before long the millers and moths and flying bugs flutter
Around the lights outside, beyond the shutters.

The first evening star shows itself
Winking at us from its shelf.
More and more stars do gradually appear,
Midnight approaches, is drawing nearer.

Clouds go drifting, lazily by
Making imaginary patterns in the sky.
The moon casts its light out through the dark.
Making curious images on the grass in the park.

The dew looks like diamonds sprinkled on the grass
Dawn creeps in and another night has passed.
The birds awake and start their chirping.
The cycle starts over, ever working.

Nights come and go,
Sometimes peaceful, sometimes slow.
But, always passing steadily on,
Bringing with it, the new dawn

(Published in *Our World's Favorite Poems Who's Who in Poetry*, The National Library of Poetry 1993, p. 78.)

New Season "Sprinter"

Sprinter has arrived!
We'll be lucky to survive.
Wind, rain, hail, ice, and snow;
All in one day, you know.
Accumulations might be large.
Mother Nature needs to take charge.
Say, "Enough!" to cold and snow.
Let the plants begin to grow.
Bring out the sun.
Tell winter it is done!
Make way for summer fun!
She must get this point across,
Or summer, too, will be totally lost.

A Mouthy Experience

Three months have gone past since a decision was made;
To remove what teeth I had left.
The decision was yes, what else could it be?
For the teeth still remaining were no good to me.
There were aches, breaks and cracks;
So take them all out at once? I asked.
Yes, was the answer, that's the very best way!
Get my teeth ready then, I have to say!
We measured and fiddled, filled my mouth with gunk.
The end result should be really quite punk.
Wait and see was the only answer I faced.
They looked good in the hand, would they in place?
The doctors were super, so were the staff.
Under I went for their removal, the time went by fast.
I like my new teeth, and how they look,
Even had thoughts of writing a book.
I thoroughly believe your attitude
Gives you an edge and latitude,
To handle a little hurt and discomfort,
When the end result is worth the effort.

Just think, forevermore;
No more drills, or novocaine and toothache pains.
I can visit the Dentist, doing what's the very easiest,
Take out my teeth, Hand them over;
And just say,
Fix it!

(This poem was published in *The Sound of Poetry Collection*, Eber and Wein Publishing, 2001–2002.)

At the Table

Are you going to be the one
Who doesn't learn from this tale
Of the people who play
All night and all day,
And their stories of woes and frustration
As they sit and test fate... at the table?

They're from all walks of life—
Girls, boys, husbands and wives,
Professionals, laborers, and poor folk—
All explaining their cards are no joke.
With the expression on faces of hope
As they tell of their expertise... at the table.

The game has become a crutch, as such,
Because they play and then complain so much
Of the goings-on of the other players.
What is this one's dreams
Becomes another's sad screams
As they go head-to-head... at the table.

Think once about just checking.
Think twice about betting.
Think thrice about now calling.
Holy cow, to even be able to raise
Takes courage, contradiction, and praise
Of how you play your cards... at the table.

Just beware if you come.
And be prepared to succumb
To the wiles of the other players
When the cards are dealt
And all bets hit the felt
As you go round and round, at the table.

If you lose all you brought
It might be for naught.
'Cause tomorrow you'll be back at it.
Lessons seem not to be learned
By the cards on the turn
That don't fit in your hand... at the table.

So do you learn from the past
That the money disappears fast?
The lesson learned: there's always a winner and loser!
So poker just for fun
Should be the aim of everyone
As you sit and test fate... at the table.

Poker Players

Once upon a time,
In a little resort town,
There was a group of players—
Carpenters and old men,
Real estate agents, bricklayers.
There were more professions, too,
But these were just a few
Who got together now and then
To sit around the table
And give the cards a spin.

They liked to play
A card game known as hold 'em.
Some played really well.
Some played and were beholdin'
To the others that were better
Or thought they knew the letter
Of the rules of the game.

They all came to try their luck,
Trying to make that extra buck
To add to their coffers.
But most find out,
After words and a pout,
That fate has a hand in the dealing.

They come together, rant and rave,
Scream, shout, and sometimes pray
To get the best hand possible,
To win the pot most profitable,
And go home a winner with the money.
While others don't think it's quite so funny.

Either way, it doesn't matter
Because they'll all be back,
No matter what they think their plight,
To return and play another night.

The Poker Game

(For all the poker players out there.)

The poker game,
A mighty one,
Packed with unknowns
And lots of fun.
You will hear words
During the play
Like "river," "flop,"
"Turn," and, "broadway."
These words are there
To make you yearn
To ante in chips.
Then wait your turn,
Only to throw in and fold
Or get the burn.
Your hand looks good.
You make a bet.
But on the flop,
No cards you get.
The turn is no better,
Not the right letter.

The river, though,
Does its job.
You bet, you call,
You lose it all!
One thing is clear
About this game of chance:
Those who fold
Or those who stay
Will be back to play
Another day!

Retirement Age

Retirement age—
Can't wait to turn that page
On our lives.
Looking forward to
All the new things to do
To keep us busy.
Kids, grandkids' involvements,
The unknown installments
Of things to come.
Health issues,
Carrying around canes and tissues
To get through the day.
Glasses to read with,
Teeth to eat with,
Pills to keep us going.
All the thrills
And the doctoring skills
To help us from knowing
The retirement years
Are not calming our fears
Of the getting closer to "going".
It's a scary thought
That things are done for naught,
And the end is nearing.

Retirement age,
One foot in the grave.
Doing nothing but fading
Except for our memories.
So make them worthwhile
For friends, lovers, and child
'Cause that's all that's left
When we leave this earth
And return to ashes and dirt
After retirement age.

Sharing Oneself

The path to a heart
Can be dangerous and long.
It can be followed
But only by the strong.
Not strong-willed or
Like lifting weights,
But by a strong personality
With loving traits!
You have to have patience,
And you have to endure.
You have to be considerate,
And you have to make sure,
You are thinking of others—
Their feelings, their likes,
Their hopes and dreams.
Realize they are unique.
Like that fact, and think
About them and not yourself.
The two of you together,
Offering each other help!
This goes for friendship also
For you have to be friends

To offer your heart
And to make amends,
As friends need to do
From time to time to stay true.
Because some people are in the dark,
Clueless about giving, sharing, and caring
All about themselves, selfish and daring.

Friendship, love, family, and such;
If you don't have these things,
Then you don't have much!
Learn to care, share, and yes, worry
About the others in your life,
Then your life is worth living!
Then you will have love in family and friends.
That's all that really matters
When we all get to the end.

Snow, Wind, Ice, and Sleet

Snow, wind, ice, sleet;
Make a difference under our feet.
In snow, we lift and plod to get through.
In ice, we try not to slip and slide.
With sleet we try to stay inside,
And wind just makes the cold seem colder.
The degrees go down as we get older.
The frost makes everything shiny and bright,
Clean, fresh, renewed, and all white.
Sometimes I wish we were in the South
When the wind blows strong, and it's cold throughout.
But then I'd miss all the shoveling and digging,
Along with the slipping and sliding.
Snow, wind, ice, and sleet,
Yeah right!
Give me the South; at least
It would be warmer out!

Summer Heat, Summer Fun, Summer Love, Summer Sun

Summer heat,
Summer fun,
Summer love,
Summer sun,
Days spent swimming, riding bikes.
Walking, running, taking hikes.
Watching stars twinkle high.
Sunsets, moonbeams, lazy nights.
Lightning bugs, picnic lunches,
Fairs and craft shows, flowers in bunches.
Green grass, cut hay, fresh breezes,
Suntans, warmth, and ice-cream freezes.
Evening walks, bare feet,
Toes wiggling in the sand and heat.
Moonlight walks,
Long talks,
Eyes locked,
No clocks,
Spent with friends,
Summer's end.

School begins.
Clothes shopping,
Shoes that fit,
Winter coats and lots of lists.
School bell rings, in our seats,
Ready for our friends to meet.
Teachers tell us time to learn,
No more summertime to burn.
Knuckle down, open the books,
Longing for just one look.
Football season,
Run and punt.
Halloween and
Time to hunt.
Thanksgiving, pumpkins, fall harvest,
Thankful for all that's best—
Family, friends, and all the rest.

Winter snow,
Icy wind, and such.
Stay inside,
Not doing much.
Winter snow,
Winds that blow,
Icy lakes and streams,
Warmer weather dreams.

Spring arrives.
Balmy breezes,
Greenery thrives.
No more freezes.

Lighter sweaters warm our backs.
Baseballs thrown and bats that crack,
Soccer league, scrapes, and bruises,
Rollerblades, wagons, and cruises.
Root beer floats,
Riding in boats
Holding hands,
Walks in the sand.
Now we've come again full circle.

Summer heat, summer fun, summer love, summer sun.

Take Time

Have you ever stopped to see
The beauty of a tree?

Or clouds floating by,
Making pictures in the sky?

Look at a blooming flower in a yard.
For it, surviving has been hard.

Or the green all around in the spring
Because it's what the showers bring.

Things happening all around us
That we should take the time to notice.

There is beauty everywhere
If we take the time to share.

Let the wonders fill our hearts.
That would be a very good start!

Take the time to see it all.

Tale of a Hiney

Here's a quick ditty,
Although not too witty,
Of a tale of a hiney.

A mom had a thought
To watch movies from the top
Of her son's bunk bed.

He helped her up
But then found she was stuck
After the movie had ended.

He was helping her down
When he had to frown
For he saw her rear "raw."

The nightgown got caught,
And he became distraught
At seeing what he saw.

"You're banned from my room
To watch movies, and soon
I hope to be over this trauma.

So go to your own bed,
Cover up your head,
And try to stop all the drama."

It now seems humorous,
But I know he was furious
Because mom was still laughing.

Thoughts about My Birthday and Thanksgiving

On Thanksgiving,
Happy birthday to me.
Boy, am I glad I'm not twenty-three.
Nor forty, for that matter.
If I went back, I'd be mad as a hatter.
I'm content to be the age that I am.
For most things, knowing that I can
Still think, that my mind is in good senses.
But my knees will no longer climb fences.
I don't really keep house like I used to.
Things aren't always done; they're, "to do."
But all in all, it's not going so badly,
Except for those that think of me madly.
Then there are those who believe I'm a little crazy.
Heck, that's better than pushing up daisies.
Because it's also Thanksgiving, I'm thankful.
So a toast to me on my birthday,
Even though I have to share it with turkeys!

Through the Years

I've tried and tried
To put in perspective
The days of our lives.
I've found no exact reason
Things happen as they do.
I did find, though,
To your own heart be true
Is the rule to follow
Most of the time,
As long as you don't hurt
Others along the line,
On your journey
Through life's mysteries,
Trying to complete
Our own life histories.
So what's the answer?
What are the stakes?
Do we really leave
Our lives to fate?
No, is the answer.
Get moving!
Put yourself in gear.

Make those resolutions!
For the upcoming year,
Set up some goals,
No matter how small.
You can get going.
You can do it all.
It just takes some gumption
Drawn from within us.
Some mindset
To say, "Get with it!"
Try your hardest,
And work at it.
And you'll be what you want
And all you can be
If you set your head and your heart
To say, "Look, I can! This is me!"
Be happy with that,
And try with all your might.
Then and only then
Will all things work out right!
So the moral is
We have the power within us
To step up to the starting line.
Go for it, and then finish!

'Tis the Season

'Tis the season; our hearts are filled with joy.
We look forward to seeing our girls and boys.
Parents, relatives, families, and friends
Gather this season to see the end
Of the last year, with its ups and downs,
And all the changes going around.
Looking back and then ahead,
Hoping nothing comes to dread.
That all goes well for everyone,
And we all get to have some fun.
Hoping for all to have good health,
Also to all, prosperity and wealth,
Family peace, and love and joy.
What more could be asked while staying coy?
Possibly make new friends
And make your amends,
So your life can become a simple plan.
Of wishing each other good health and cheer,
Making it good for all to have a great New Year.

What Can Be Done for Their Grandson?

They have a grandson,
And I feel so bad
That he's hurting so much
And reacting so sadly
To all the misfortunes he thinks are in his life
Making his reactions mad!
If we could only make him realize
All things will get better
And will pass.
But, of course, he doesn't think so,
So our words don't mean crap.
What to do to get him to understand
That his reaction to things
Is not acceptable behavior?
Nothing seems to work,
Nothing in our favor.
All we can do is try
With patience and understanding.
But they have to admit
They find it hard to resist paddling!
He screams, pushes, throws, and barricades himself in,
Not realizing that none of these things
Help his case to win.

He tries to hurt all in his path.
No respect, no tolerance, no class.
Family's a target for throws and fists.
Everyone else blamed for most things
That happen to him,
Not realizing his own words and actions
Lead him further down the path of destruction.
How to get through that thick head?
We all, every one of us, have this dread:
If he doesn't shape up and get rid of his attitude,
There will be no choice left for anyone.
No leeway, no latitude.
He'll be doomed to a life
Without friends, family, loving, and caring.
Not a soul who'll want to be a friend.
No parents helping to the end.
The bridges all will be burned
If he continues down this path of no return!

Where and When?

There was once a young girl
Moved with her family to a new world.
There was a certain young boy who lived up the hill.
He said, "One day I'll have that girl, I will."

He did as he said he would.
They dated and saw each other when they could.
Then they parted ways, not knowing exactly why.

Both thought of each in the years gone by.
And fifty-seven years later, caught each other's eyes.
They conversed for months and got along fine.
Like no time had passed in all that time.

They could talk for hours, no topic off limits.
Like time hadn't lapsed, and they were still "with it."
They got along fine on all those long conversations
But had not had a chance to see each other in person.

Sometimes they thought it might get mapped in.
Then something would come up, and they couldn't make it again!
Fate had a hand in their lives, they are sure!
But what the heck! What's the cure?

How and when does all this interference end,
And they get a say on their fates in time left to spend?
They're not getting younger as each month passes.
Will they get days together before time turns them to ashes?

They are best friends, but will it become more?
Only time will tell if they can get through that door
To a new chapter, one with both still fit.
Or will time tell if this is meant to be it?

'Twas a Week and a Month before Christmas

'Twas a week and a month before Christmas.
And all was *not* well.
Plans were not coming together.
Things were going to ----.
Our fiftieth anniversary was first.
No worries, went smoothly and quiet.
Dinner together and then a movie.
Dinner we got, movie not!
The parking lot was overflowing.
The week of Thanksgiving,
My birthday first.
I told them no cakes!
The candles would burn down the place.
Cakes there were, two of them.
And also pumpkin bars and apple crisp!
No wonder I look like this!
So next day, our son's birthday.
More cake and trinity food
To set the pace and the mood
For eating Thanksgiving dinner.

All five of us were here,
With four more to add to the cheer,
To give thanks for all we have,
Whether it be good or bad.
Thanksgiving evening a new twist;
Cynthia and Grandma had a wish
To go shopping on Black Friday eve.
Cynthia wanted to see
What all the hype was about.
Well, we found out!
Packed like sardines,
Could hardly move through the aisles.
Not many people had on their smiles.
Some were downright rude.
Patience was lost on most of these dudes!
Cynthia was brave
For the very next day,
She went with Aunt T
To Sioux Falls to see
Black Friday in person!
She said it wasn't too bad,
And the time they had
Was okay but didn't get enough
Shopping time in
Before they had to come home again—
At 1:30 in the morning—
And then get up
And work the next morning!
All weekend long we had
The turkey and ham,
Plus all those cakes, pies, and such
Leftover from Thanksgiving, too much!
So much good food, I've sprung a leak!
Now we're in December.

Maybe things will slow.
Christmas lights will glow.
All over, everyone has up lights,
Making evenings all colors and bright.
Cold is coming; so is snow.
Why I am not in the South
Is what I'd like to know!
Shopping is coming up.
I don't enjoy it quite as much
As when the children were little.
The pleasure in watching their faces,
The wonder and awe
At everything they see in those places.
Santa's timely return with presents
Or possibly coal—
Only the person themselves know
Which one will show.
Kids playing in the snow,
Coming in for hot chocolate.
Singing Christmas tunes,
Shaking packages under the tree.
Oh, how I wish it could be
Those simple times again.
Without the hectic hypes and spins,
An easygoing, enjoyable time
Of simple holiday pleasures with
Family and friends of mine!

Peace, love, and happiness to all,
and to all a good night.

POEMS
AND IDEAS
FOR SPECIAL OCCASIONS
FOR FRIENDS,
FAMILY
AND ARPOKI
WOMENS CLUB

First Aid Kits For Any Age, Birthday, Retirement, Joke for Younger, gag gift....................

Gather items and put in a wrapped container

Use list to write out what they're for.....All of these or only a few...

Pencil. To get the lead out
Buttons. To button down the hatch
Tacks. To keep you sharp
Needle and Thread. Mending you together when you feel like you are falling apart.
Rubber Bands. When you are stretched to the limit.
Little Bow. For your finger to help you remember what you forgot or when you can't remember shit!
Matches. To keep your flame from going out or light a fire under you.
String. To keep your act together, or stop you from falling apart.
Rope. To add when you are at the end of yours.
Safety Pins. To hold you together when you are bursting at the seams.
Hooks and Eyes. To help you see better.
Ball. To bounce back from whatever comes your way.
Marbles. For when you lose yours and can't locate them

Nuts. For where you are going or to join the club...nuts as in nuts and bolts type nuts.

File. To help you stay organized, or get out when they lock you up. Fingernail type of file.

Bandaids. To mend or pull yourself back together.

Batteries. For when you are running low you can charge yourself up.

Most of these things we all have in a drawer or sewing kit or in our garage, so you don't have to run out and get something; you already have these things probably.

Have fun with it!!

Karen (Taylor) Ritzer

Template for First Aid Kit
to put in with items

This is your, _____ Birthday, first aid kit
Made to help you stay fit.
Keep it handy, in a safe place.
You never know when it will help with the race.
Some of these things you may have had
But didn't know you needed them so bad!
In case you forget what all these things were made for;
The reminder below, will help get you out the door.

Needle and thread ...when you feel you're coming apart at the seams

Ball... to help you bounce back

Pencil and note paper...to help remember what you forget

Rubber bands..... When you are feeling sluggish, helps you snap back

Batteries....when you need a charge because yours are run down

Coupon.... When you think you're running out of gas

Safety pins....when you're falling apart

Marbles...when you swear you've lost yours

Extra rope .....when you think you're at the end of yours...add this on

String...when you are fit to be tied

Tacks. ...to help you stay sharp

A pair of extra eyes ...to help you find lost things

Glue ...for, of course, when you become unglued!

All for you, _____

OUR HAPPY BIRTHDAY WISH ....

IS THAT FOR MANY TEARS TO COME,
YOU WILL NEVER NEED ANY OF THIS.!!!!!!

YOUR FRIENDS,

_____

Arpoki Women's Club

Meeting at City Hall
1st Wednesday every month

December 2009,

Dear Fiends,

HAPPY HOLIDAYS

Happy Holidays to all.
Let our meeting begin.

It's Christmas time...
Forget being thin!!

The snow can wait
Until Christmas Eve;

So travelers may drive
With care and ease.

Shopping...OH, WHAT GLORIOUS FUN!
Hitting all the sales, while on the run.

Parties are delightful
With goodies and such;

Of course, we all indulge
Way too much!....

Children are preparing for Santa's arrival.
All adults are thinking of... is survival!!

Christmas songs are playing wherever we go;
Floating up from CD's, MP3's and stereos.

The season is wonderful and filled with glee.
Especially when shared with all of our friends... in ARPOKI.

Karen Rae Ritzer

December Arpoki Meeting 2016

Our Christmas Party was a blast!
Shannon's new house, we all saw at last.
On East lake with a terrific view,
Everything freshly painted, polished and new.

We all found our way bearing presents for kids.
And the hostesses fed us and served us, THEY DID!!

We played a new made up game,
You got a present if you could name,
The correct answer, if to you it came.
Then if you got it correct
You got a present of jewelry to unwrap.
Or you could take from someone else's stack.

We had a good time, with lots of laughs
And the bonus was, we learned some new facts.
Then the time came to say goodnight
We thanked all and departed into the light.

The weather held, we all got home safely,
Most fun we'd all had lately.
Merry Christmas to all, was the verse heard mainly...
But, wait, was it us ?? No..
It was from the rooftop quite plainly!!!!!!!

Merry Christmas To All
And To All A Good Night!

Karen Ritzer

Arpoki Ditty

There once was a girl from DOVER
Who invited her boyfriend _____   over
And when he arrived LATE
He put his trust in _____   fate
He got down on one _____   knee
And hoped that _____   she
Would say yes to his QUARRY
So then they could _____   marry
Living happily ever after.

There once was a girl from SPAIN
who had a very bad _____   strain
Everywhere she had to _____   hop
Even if she was going to _____   shop
So her groceries she had to MOP

There was a boy from CHINA
He worked very hard in a _____   diner
At the end of his SHIFT
He created a _____   dish
The patrons thought was just FINA

Have fun, putting in your own rhyming words.

Karen Ritzer

Arpoki Christmas
December 6, 2017

Twas the night of Arpoki Christmas,
And all through the town;
Snowflakes were falling, down, down, down.
I, in my coat, and you in your boots
Had just walked in to see the cat and dog cut loose!
Running, twisting and leaping and such
The scene was exciting but, a little bit much,
To take all in, What a sight,
We hope this doesn't go on all night!
Wanda was chasing the dog with a stick,
Helen was giving the frosting a lick.
And Peggy in her nightgown, and Lavonne in her cap,
Were patiently waiting for presents to unwrap.
When, all of a sudden, Theresa called out,
Everyone come take a look!!
Even Ginger stopped reading, putting down her book.
And we all went to see the sight
It was Shannon, about to get in the fight.
"NO, don't hit the snowman", Pam yelled out loudly.
While Marilyn, swung hard, quite proudly!
Snow flew all over while Beth took a deep breath,
Before trying to find the pieces that were left.
Martha, hurried to help find a nose and an eye;

While Linda kept her eyes on the baking pies.
Sally was busy setting the table just so, And Julie was pouring the glasses of wine.
So, Pat made sure we all heard, "it's Dinner time".
We all ran back inside as the phone was ringing
It was Theresa Danne wishing us all Merry Christmas in singing.
Then after eating potluck and stuffing ourselves like a duck.
We turned to BINGO and tried our luck!
When we got a bingo, We all got a gift,
Some liked theirs, some thought they were stiffed!
So all in all, it was a good evening of food and fun,
And we all departed for home saying to all and leaving out none;
While watching Santa cross the sky on his midnight flight;
MERRY CHRISTMAS TO ALL .....AND TO YOU ALL, A GOOD NIGHT!!!!!!!

Karen Ritzer

Butterfly Club

You've heard of the Red Hat Club and what they are about.
Well, I am a member of the Butterfly Club
Hence, the reason for my Fashion statement.
It is my Butterfly Suit
Representing our constantly changing stages of life!

At our different ages in time, we come out of our cacoons
And emerge into our next stage of life.
Pursuing our new adventures and challenges.

Moving on and showing our resiliency
with whatever comes our way
We are all butterflies, individuals, no
two alike, beautiful and ever
changing.
Welcome
Because we are all members of the Butterfly Club

Karen Rae (Taylor) Ritzer
This was for a meeting of our Ladies Arpoki Club
For this little demonstration, I had a see through webbed
material and made it into
wings pinned on my arms.....so as I spoke I went from normally
dressed to raising
my arms out slowly as I read my spiel, and walla' at the finish, I
had wings;
So, I emerged as a butterfly.
That's was how I made my point.

ARPOKI = Arnolds Park Okoboji Ladies
Club, started in the 1950s

Come Visit With Me (Lissa) At The Kurio Kastle Pottery Shop

COME VISIT WITH ME
MY NAME IS LISSA
COME IN AND I'LL SHOW
YOU WHAT YOU'RE MISSIN'

COME VISIT WITH ME
IT WILL CALM YOUR MIND
MAKE SOMETHING UNIQUE
ONE OF A KIND

PICK SOMETHING OUT
AND TAKE YOUR TIME
DECORATE IT IN ANY WAY
IT'S JUST TIME IN YOUR DAY

YOU'LL HAVE LOTS OF FUN
WHILE GETTING IT DONE
I'LL EVEN GLAZE AND FIRE YOUR OBJECT
YOU MAY KEEP OR GIFT AWAY YOUR PROJECT

SO, COME ON IN
PUT ON A GRIN
VISIT WITH RICKY
DON'T HAVE TO BE PICKY

IT'S TIME WELL SPENT
AND WILL BE PERMANENT
THE WHOLE FAMILY CAN PARTAKE
AND YOU GET A CHERISHED KEEPSAKE!!!

clay and pottery making, you paint and Lissa glazes it and fires it
for you.

By Karen Rae (Taylor) Ritzer

Elizabeth and Jonathon For Wedding (and For First Christmas)

CONGRATULATIONS

Some words of advise on your Wedding Day
ALWAYS REMEMBER
As you start your life together
Never, ever, go to sleep mad at each other!
Remember communication and respect
And all will turn out for the best.
Keep your romance alive
Take no one for granted, and it will survive.
Be kind, caring, and sharing
And you will be the perfect pairing.
Lastly, never say goodbye without a kiss
Practice these things and you life together can be bless!
Best wishes to you both for now and always!!

KAREN

Inside their Wedding gift, is a clear glass Christmas Ornament
Ball for their First Christmas Tree, with this message

My wish for you as your journey begins
Is that the love you have now, Never Ends
You'll have ups and downs, like most couples do,
But, the love will hold and get you through.
There will be good, There will be bad;
Don't ever, ever go to sleep being mad
Communication will always be
The way to fix things and is the key!
As your new life together starts
I wish you the Fairy Tale Life,
With all my heart!!

Karen (Taylor) Ritzer

Helen and Dale

Happy under the sun
Have had each other
For seventy and one.

There for one another
Thru' thick and thin.
They will tell you
How happy they have been.

We salute your stamina,
Also your love enduring
And hope your future years together
Will not be boring!

Our wish is that you will reach
the number twenty-five times three
Still enjoying and loving each other merrily!!!!

Best Wishes & Congratulations
Happy 71st Anniversary Helen and Dale

Karen and Tom Ritzer

Jeopardy Okoboji Style #1

1. This building was a train depot and major dance pavilion.

_____

2. Some of the activities inside this space were the barrel and slide

_____

3. One of our members had a business across from this original hotel/golf course _____

4. It was a variety store on Broadway where Yesterdays is now.

_____

5. A former members Hardware store used to be located in the building that was originally a _____

6. Buds Grocery store was on the hwy. in Arnolds Park, the small area next to it was _____

7. Amy's Sign Design used to be _____

8. What building housed the critters and huge turtle, later causing controversies _____

9. Before it was the Ritz, and the Crossings this was _____

10. The Rest Haven was under this well known landmark _____

11. Before KFC and Then the Wharf, It was one of the oldest structures still here. _____

12. This building was home to the survivor of an Indian raid and massacre _____

13. This building housed the first buffet in the area on the old hwy 71 road to Milford _____

14. This Pocahontas point building had a great view and restraunt

_____

15. Which club is one of the longest running in Arnolds Park.

_____

16. This Author penned Okoboji and Murder in Okoboji

_____

17. This family probably has the youngest (and cutest) accomplished musicians in Arnolds Park _____

18. This local Author of three books has been to our club as a guest speaker _____

Karen (Taylor) Ritzer

Jeopardy Okoboji Style #2
Fall 2012

1. This was the first place in the Lakes area to bring us Mexican cuisine _____

2. I was located under the Roof Garden, (not the fun house) but children still liked me. _____

3. In the first half of the 20th century my life was going fast on top of the lake water and then, alas, for the last half it was spent under the water _____

4. I used to have people come to eat, now I house a previous club members insurance business. _____

5. Across from the school, I sold a lot of candy to children on their way home and some gas _____

6. Before I became a "pair of dice", I washed things. _____

7. This was my stomping grounds with narratives of our history as an extra while you road me, I'm no longer in the lake area.

_____

8. There used to be peanuts on my floor (before it became the in thing to do) and my next door neighbor had music and go go girls in the sixties. _____

9. There was a certain color to my name, as I sat on another corner across from the school. _____

10. You could watch the boat and car traffic while eating here. Then probably walk to your mobile home _____

11. If you liked music and horses, I was on a strip of land east of the main amusement park _____

12. My name should remind you of police, but lovers liked me too in the old days _____

13. Between the Tabernacle, and Ruebins area I sat waiting for use from vets. _____

Karen (Taylor) Ritzer

Jeopardy Okoboji Style
Answers to page 1 and 2

page 1
1. Central Emporium
2. The Fun House
3. Dee
4. Elloween's
5. Consumer's Lumber yard
6. Arnolds Park Dry Cleaners
7. Arnolds Park City Hall
8. Kurio Kastle
9. Gregerson's Resort
10. The Roof Garden
11. Okoboji Store and Bait shop
12. Gardner Cabin
13. Log Cabin
14. Vern & Coilas
15. Arpoki Women's Club
16. Peter Davidson
17. Alexanders
18. Teresa Jones

page 2
1. The Taco House
2. The Rest Haven Arcade
3. The Thriller
4. Walker's Insurance
5. Thompson's Gas Station
6. Walkers Car Wash
7. The Empress
8. The Peacock
9. Red's Cafe
10. O'Farell Sisters
11. The Merry Go Round
12. Stakeout Road
13. The Legion Hall

Megan's Bridal Shower

We thought and thought
Just could not think!
What to bring Megan
To make her that shade of pink
She gets when she's embarrassed,
Or can't quite think
What to respond with
When others' words make her "blink".

So, hence part of this gift
Meant to make her blush;
And after the wedding
I hopefully become flushed!

The other part is because....
When asked what she needed,
Her very quick response was;
"We really don't need anything.
But, cash would be great!"
She made it so easy
For us to follow her dictate.

Happy Bridal Shower, Megan
Brought to Rich, by FATE!!!

Karen & Tom

Pam

Happy Seventy Fifth Birthday
We are so Happy to be here for your 75th Birthday
To help you celebrate Three Quarters of a Century!
To remind you of all the the years you have enjoyed,
And shared with the people in your life.
We all want to Thank you, on Your Day,
For Being in our lives.
Knowing you has made all of us better people.
Happier and kinder people, following your example.
We all wish you nothing but Sunshine, Love and Happiness,
For all your coming Years.
Thank You from all of US for being YOU!!!
HAPPY 75th BIRTHDAY PAM
You Deserve The Best
WE ALL LOVE YOU!!!!

Peggy

How wonderful that you have been,
Here ninety years with all your friends.
We love to see that special smile,
And so glad to know you for awhile.
Your conversations are so fun!
We all enjoy listening to every one!!
The life stories you can tell;
Are so special to us, and well.....
We're just so glad that you are here
So we can help you celebrate this year!
Keep up your faith and GOD willin';
On your hundredth we'll all be chillin'.

See you then!!!!!!

Karen

Rhonda and Larry's Wedding

TO: RHONDA, LARRY AND FAMILY
A POEM FOR YOUR DAY

YOU HAD YOURS,
AND YOU HAD MINE;
AND FOR AWHILE
THINGS WERE FINE.
THEN WE MET.
AND HOW THINGS CHANGED.
OUR LIVES FIT TOGETHER,
WE WERE REARRANGED.
ALL FOR THE GOOD
OF EVERYONE CONCERNED.
OUR FAMILIES CAME TOGETHER
AND FOR THE BETTER.
OUR BOYS AND GIRL
GET ALONG GREAT.
OUR FAMILY GREW,
WITH THE LOVE AND CARING OF WE TWO.
SO, IT COMES TO NOW,
THE RECITING OF ALL OUR VOWS.

TWO FAMILIES COMBINED,
WITH LOVE, CARING, AND
UNDERSTANDING IN MIND;
TO FOREVER SHARE,
ALL THEIR LIVES TOGETHER,
FOREVER ENTWINED
AS ONE.

HAPPINESS AND LOVE TO YOU ALWAYS
AUNT KAREN AND UNCLE TOM

A
COUPLE OF SONG
LYRICS

Song
The moon up above
fall 1962

The moon up above,
Shines brightly for my love
It shines because our love is meant to be.

The stars up above,
Twinkle for my love
I'm wishing that he was here with me.

The lightning bugs at night,
Flash for the life
The life we will together share and see.

The first star I see tonight,
Watch over my loves life,
Don't let him go astray from me.

I love him tonight,
I will all of my life
Please let him feel the same about me.

The darkness at night
It is just right

For two people in love to be together.

The wind blows free
He's coming now to me
So we'll always be together and believe;

No matter where we are
We can look to the stars
And see each others love in the light.

Oh Darlin' can't you see
We were meant to be
So, hold me tight, all through the nights and ALWAYS....

Karen Rae Taylor.   Fall '62 first love

Song
I've Fallen In Love
winter 1962-63

I've fallen in love with you my dear,
I'm loving you all the while.
You're perfect whatever you do,
But I love you best when you smile.

I've fallen in love, so deeply in love,
And I'm hoping that you have too.
I've fallen in love with you my dear,
I've fallen in love with you.

The look in your eyes, I demise,
Tells me, you love me too.
Our love feels so perfectly right
with the stars overhead out so bright.

Can we endure, as life passes by,
And as lovers through the years
Hopefully we will forever be you and I
Always together and still in love my dear

I love you tonight,
I will all of my life.
Tell me you feel the same about us too.

Karen Rae Taylor

Oh, Lucifer Oh, Lucifer 2014-16

Bob B.   2014
How's this so far? Or were you looking to have another direction
for him????

Oh Lucifer Oh Lucifer
what happened to you?
why did you drop from favor?
what made you split from the savior?

did you fall from his graces
for not singing his praises?
or did you plan your evil years
from day one, based on evil fears.

is hell really that great
to seal mere mortals fates
to an after life of hell
for their wrong doing of well...?

Oh Lucifer Oh Lucifer
why the temptations and trials
why the conceit and denials
to gain or take a soul
for yourself to have control.

what was your goal, even then
did you know so many would sin

would have thoughts of hate and deceit
would have contempt for others, head to feet?

control of the world, through wicked ways
seems to be your main stay
to throw the souls into the fray
bringing on what it may.

Oh Lucifer Oh Lucifer
you're such a hate filled kind of guy
we could break you if we knew why;
you wanted this world to be in your hands
all of us need to say no to your plans.

you would lose all your power
if all of us would not cower
and use our endevers in life
to end all human strife.

we could have love and kindness
lead us all away from your badness
saving the world from sadness
and into the light of His kindness.

Oh Lucifer Oh Lucifer
how great to have your days numbered
Everyone at peace, unencumbered
So the world could be free
to treat each other with compassion and love
As it was meant to be.

Oh Lucifer Oh Lucifer
To hell with you!!!!!!!!!!

by, Karen Rae (Taylor) Ritzer started 2014

AN
ORIGINAL
POEM I WROTE
FOR MY
GRANDCHILDREN
AND IS NOW
AN ILLUSTRATED
CHILDREN'S BOOK
"OFF TO DREAMLAND"

Off TO DREAMLAND ORIGINALLY WRITTEN BY KAREN RITZER IN 1999 FOR OUR GRANDCHILDREN, NICHOLAS AND CYNTHIA

WE CAN GO TO CALIFORNIA
SEE THE SAN DIEGO ZOO
ROUND THE SIERRA MOUNTAINS
SEE THE PACIFIC OCEAN TOO.

WE CAN STOP AT DISNEYLAND
AND PLAY ALL DAY
TAKE A TRIP TO AUSTRALIA
AND JUST FLY AWAY

WE DON'T NEED A PLANE
JUST OUR ARMS WILL DO
IN OUR DREAMS, YOU AND I
CAN DO ANYTHING WE WANT TO.

WE CAN BUILD A CASTLE
IN THE SWISS ALPS
RAISE DOGS IN GERMANY

SEND THEM OUT TO HELP
FIND LOST SKIERS AS THEY SCHLOALUM
GO TO ROME TO SEE THE COLUMNS

HEAR BIG BEN IN LONDON
AND SEE BUCKINGHAM PALACE
DRIVING ON THE WRONG SIDE
WITHOUT A THOUGHT OF MALICE

KISS THE IRISH BLARNEY STONE
AND JUMP THE FJORDS OF SCOTLAND
WE CAN DO ALL OF THIS
WHILE SLEEPING ON SHEETS OF COTTON..

WE COULD GO TO RUSSIA
SEE THE CZARS
END UP IN TOKYO, JAPAN
PULLING RICK- SHAWS

SAIL THE OCEAN IN A YACHT
GO TO SAILING SCHOOL
LEARN TO TIE ALL THE KNOTS
AND ALL THE NAUTICAL RULES
GO TO THE MOON AND BACK

AND BE AN ASTRONAUT
BRING THE SHUTTLE BACK TO EARTH
AND REST IT IN IT'S BERTH
THEN TRAVEL ON A TRAIN
TO RIDE THE TRACKS TO PERTH.

SO, DON'T WORRY IF WE HAVE TO PART
FOR A VERY SHORT TIME.
A LITTLE WHILE HERE AND THERE
WILL NOT BREAK OUR HEARTS.

WE CAN SEE EACH OTHER ALL WE WANT
WHEN WE ARE NOT NEAR
BY THINKING HARD, CLOSING OUR EYES
AND DREAMING OF EACH OTHER.
IN OUR DREAMS WE WILL MEET
EVERY NIGHT, AND DISCOVER
ALL THE WONDERS OF THE WORLD
AND SOME NOT EVEN KNOWN YET,
CAUSE YOU AND I WILL ALWAYS
BE ADVENTURERS TOGETHER,
IN OUR DREAMS WE CAN MEET
AND BE WHATEVER WE WISH TO
GOODNIGHT, SLEEP TIGHT, AND SEE YOU
IN OUR DREAMS...............

DON'T FRET LITTLE ONE
WHEN WE HAVE TO PART
FOR YOU AND I CAN SEE EACH OTHER
ANYTIME WE WANT
JUST CLOSE YOUR EYES
AND START TO DREAM
AND WE CAN BE ANYWHERE
DOING THINGS WE'VE NEVER DONE
SHOWING THAT WE CARE.
JUST REACH OUT
AND TAKE MY HAND
AND OFF WE GO
AWAY TO DREAMLAND

FROM RUSSIA ON REVISED FOR BOOK 5-30-19
WE COULD GO TO RUSSIA, TO SEE THE CZARS
END UP IN TOKYO, JAPAN
PULLING PASSENGERS IN RICK-SHAWS

SAIL THE OCEANS ON A YACHT

THEN GO TO SAILING SCHOOL
LEARN TO TIE ALL THE KNOTS
AND ALL THE NAUTICAL RULES.

GO TO THE MOON AND BACK
BE AN ASTRONAUT, IN FACT,
WE COULD BRING THE SHUTTLE BACK TO EARTH
AND PARK IT IN IT'S OWN BERTH.
THEN WE'LL TRAVEL ON A TRAIN
RIDING THE RAILS TO PERTH.

SO, DON'T WORRY IF WE HAVE TO PART
A LITTLE WHILE HERE AND THERE,
WILL NOT BREAK OUR HEARTS.
WE CAN SEE EACH OTHER ALL WE WANT
WHEN WE ARE NOT TOGETHER,
BY THINKING HARD, CLOSING OUR EYES
AND PICTURING EACH OTHER!
IN OUR DREAMS WE WILL MEET
EVERY NIGHT, AND SOON DISCOVER
ALL THE WONDERS OF THE WORLD
'CAUSE YOU AND I WILL ALWAYS BE ADVENTURERS
TOGETHER!!!!!!

DON'T FRET LITTLE ONES, WHEN WE HAVE TO PART,
FOR YOU AND I CAN SEE EACH OTHER, IN OUR MINDS
AND HEARTS.
IN OUR DREAMS WE CAN MEET AND BE WHATEVER WE
WISH TO
GOOD NIGHT, SLEEP TIGHT, AND IN MY DREAMS I'LL
SEE YOU!!

JUST CLOSE YOUR EYES AND START TO DREAM
AND WE CAN BE ANYWHERE!!
DOING THINGS WE'VE NEVER DONE

SHOWING HOW MUCH WE CARE
JUST REACH OUT AND HOLD MY HAND
AND OFF WE'LL GO, YOU AND ME
AWAY, TO DREAMLAND................................

2 MORE PARAGRAPHS WERE ADDED IN 2021
AND THE REST REVISED A LITTLE TO MAKE THE CHILDRENS BOOK
FOR PUBLISHING IN 2022. OFF TO DREAMLAND ILLUSTRATED BY
KASANDRA ABRIOLA

OUR
FIRST
RETIREMENT TRIP

This is our adventure of "Our First Retirement Trip to Texas." December 1, 2011 to April 2, 2012

To the Rio Grande Valley and to Arroyo City, On the Colorado River.
Where our first winter there we did not have to shiver.
For four months we called Bayway our home
We liked the river area, the people, the animals and sun;
And each other!! and had fun.!!!!

We did discover one thing that should be changed about retirement.
Everyone should retire from the age of 40 to 50 or so...
Then go back to work after that...
And the reasoning behind this thought...Is so that...
You can enjoy and do the things you would like to
While your body and mind can still do the things you want them to!!

Hope you enjoy our storytelling endeavor
To explain to you, how we enjoyed the weather.
As seen through our eyes

Made With Love,
Mom, Dad, Grandma, Grandpa, Tom & Karen Ritzer, relative, or friend.
Whichever Applies!!

OUR RETIREMENT TRIP TO
THE VALLEY
December 1-12, 2011

On our retirement trip to the valley,
When we left we did not dally.
We made the trip in 30 hours,
To Arroyo City, and Bayway, which will be ours;
For the next hundred and twenty days
We will enjoy fishing, and the suns rays.
We brought just what we needed to,
Not everything, but we will make do.
We have a Texas Room with a T V
Facing the river where Tom will be.
I can do beading in the Texas Room
And paint in the morning light, listening to tunes,
In the East side screened in porch
And relax at night under the Tiki torch.
We can breakfast on the West side deck
And then in the moonlight we can neck. NO?? oh, Heck!!!
If I can get Tom to quit watching news from the couch
In the living room where he likes to slouch.
The kitchen area is bright and sunny
And big enough to allow our tummies
To pass by the table that seats six,

On our way to the fridge to make a pick,
Of a cold drink or maybe a snack,
Before Tom gets another attack
Of going down to the dock to fish,
For he's doing exactly what he wished!
King, is enjoying the investigation
Of all the new smells and without hesitation.
He weathered the trip quite well,
Slept most of the way with no yells.
We got all unpacked and stored away
And intend to enjoy the next 120 days.
The saga will continue...of that I'm sure!

Now I'm waiting for the postman to appear
To tell me how the heck you get a mail box down here!
We have one restaurant in Arroyo City,
The name of it is, Chili Willies.
There are two bait shops and a country store;
And that's about it for business' for.....
Anything else you have to go into town
With gas prices...I do this with a frown.
For mail, internet, and telephone you get the run-a-round
Today we got our mailbox up and attached
Ends up, the state highway guys take care of that.
But, only after four stops here and there;
No one knew, and I don't think they care.
Now, it's there and mail can be delivered
Next up, land line, so we can call and be heard.

Wednesday brought three men to fix the path,
That Tom has to travel to fish on the dock and laugh;
At the poor souls back home contending with snow.
It almost makes us feel we shouldn't let them know...
How nice it is here and this retirement stage,
We wish everyone could to; but, at an earlier age!!

Rain has finally come to the Valley at last.
The ground is ready to soak it up fast!
Gave us some time to enjoy the Texas room
Watch boat and barge traffic and use the telescope zoom
To see what we could find on the wildlife Refuge
Across the arroyo (canal) from the dock we use.
In there, I can do beadwork, watch Tom fish and T V
All at the same time, multi-tasking you see.
The Gardner and Landscaping men are here today.
To clean and clear and haul away, so we can play!
We discovered then, we have a lime tree too.
Along with the orange, grapefruit, and lemon. To few??
I've planted some avacado seeds in the yard,
We'll see what happens, I'll send a card.
The only thing left is to actually get to painting
And, when I get to do that, they'll be no more waiting.
Everything will be, as we want it to be here.
We can sit back and enjoy a wine or a beer.
Even if it is only 2:00 in the afternoon!!!
We're sure the months will go by way to soon
Just so you all know!! We miss you each A LOT!!!
But, we sure are enjoying where we are and who we've got!!!

Thank You to you all for helping us get here.
Miss You All!!
Love You All!!
Mom, DAD, (Tom and Karen)

December 13-24, 2011

Yikes, the Gardner scalped the yard and trees...
He says it grows back quickly and helps let in the breeze.
We found out this morning,we had thieves during the night.
The scoundrels took off with Toms' fish, what a plight.
They brought the basket up out of the water;

Chewed a hole through the metal net, didn't bother,
To say thank you or whatever, but left their footprints...
In the sand, little paw prints is better, you get the hint?
They were critters, and they wore their masks!
To better accomplish their thieving task!
Not one fish was left to clean or cook;
But we learned our lesson...we will now look,
To make sure the basket is much stronger
And that it's suspended three feet into the water.

Tom got his coumadin checked and the follow-up
The appointment was for Saturday..., YUP!!!
You heard right,...The Dr. was in!!
Saturdays are normal here, that's how it's been.
We're picking some grapefruit, oranges and limes
For the next week and some juicing time.
Tom is fixing a rod holder and a latch on his box,
That holds his gear out on the dock.
So, He might not need to come to the house at all;
Till he tires to the point of throwing in the towel.
Still don't have a permanent solution for the internet.
But, I'm working on it, that you can bet!
Donna and Dick Christoffer came to visit on Sunday
Found their way here with their Garmin, but long didn't stay
They fished and visited, then went on their way
It had started to rain, putting a damper on fish play
Tonight, several boats went by on the river, between six and seven
All lit up with Christmas lights, playing songs and motors revin'
Back and forth on the river they went
Passing joy to others...time well spent.
We clapped and cheered them on,
They waved, played their Christmas songs and were gone.
Yesterday, we went to sign up Tom at the V A
Didn't know it would be such an ordeal...ALL DAY

Six hours we spent, to get a part
For that's all we needed! Nothing else at the start...
Sign in, sit, wait, see an admin person,
Sit, wait, see a nurse, then sit, wait on your buns.
Finally about to close, go to another building...
To get the part from another nurse unyielding..
So, eventually we got the part we needed;
But trying to tell them that's all we want went unheeded.
Trying again today for that internet connection
It has been a search, and avoids my detection.
Dad's going fishing because he missed yesterday
To get his line wet, to catch a fish, is why we stay!
He got a bird feeder a few days ago...
So, now we have birds and squirrels for the show
We watch them in the morning sun
Drinking our coffee on the deck, it's fun.
Talked to Tom & Evonne Smith about getting together to visit
We will meet somewhere between, just pick it!!
When the Holidays are over and complete
We'll go see their new house on the beach.

Mexico was quite safe, and the same as always,
Tom visiting the Dentist, and shopping filled our day.
Then we did...new release movies, meds, shoeshine and such
I even got a margarita, while the Dentist did his finishing touch.
We started home with our goodies in tow,
Went right through customs with nothing to declare, you know!
Ate on the way home at Chili Willies place.
The décor is simple and the food you don't waste.

December 24, 2011

Well that's brought us to Christmas Eve.
We are going nowhere and don't plan to leave.
We are settled in, for the holiday weekend.

Our love and salutations we send!!!!!!
For the first time in more years than we care to remember
Dad and I will be alone together
For Christmas Eve, I won't be busy with everything else
I can concentrate on him and myself!
For Christmas Day, we're only sorry we are not with our children and family
But it's time for their traditions to be made, and set them free
To do what they want to do on these Holidays.
SO!!!!
MERRY CHRISTMAS TO ALL!!!!!! WE LOVE YOU DEARLY!!!!
MISS YOU A LOT......... BUT....WE ARE ENJOYING THIS TIME TOGETHER
HAPPY NEW YEAR TOO!

You all are forever in our thoughts and Hearts
MOM AND DAD ....Tom and Karen

Don't worry ...more to follow....(I saw those eyes roll & heard that groan!) Love Ya

December 25th to the end of 2011

Christmas Day brought no events
Quietly the day was spent.
We talked with each one of our children,
Telling them we love and miss them...
Aunt Sharon, Bobby, Angie and Kaylee
Also called to make sure we were Merry!

It started off windy and kind of dreary
But by late afternoon it started clearing.
So guess what Tom went out to do..
No, it wasn't to go play horseshoes.
Down to the dock to fish of course,

Bet you guessed something worse??
Of course not, you all know better.
Only thing that makes him not fish, is weather!!!
Oh your Dad and I did get each other,
A gift for us, we went together
We are shareholders of some stock,
Both in agreement of what we got!
The Green Bay Packers are now winning for us.
Someday we'll go watch them, take a bus.
Hope you all had a Merry Christmas!!!!!

December 27, 2011

It has been uneventful the last couple of days.
The sun has been out and the sky a blue haze.
I am relaxing, enjoying the mornings being lazy,
Until dad gets up and then wei get ...busy.. (thought I was going to
use a different word here didn't you)
Eat a bite and have our morning java
Maybe on the wildlife refuge see a llama
Clean the fish from yesterdays catch
Fix the backdoors very loose latch.
Then Dad can go fishing some more
And I can go do what I adore.
I Just heard from Maddie, Mr. Polk is signing an OK
For us to receive internet service at this property
At least it starts the process, now they come look
To see if the satellite will let us hook
Up and stay connected for a time
If so, I'm ready to pay the dime!!!
Well, we'll have to see what they find out...
But with the way it's been going I have a doubt.
Maddie, is our realtor, she takes care of Bay Way   (that is the
                                        name of the house we're in)
Mr. Polk is the owner, who let's us all stay

At the places he owns and rents to all of us
People who come here to avoid winters fuss.
The internet tech will give us a call
When they can come and look at this all
To see if we can even receive
The broadband beams, here by the sea.
Sometime between now and January tenth,
Boy, we'll have to celebrate and have an event!
I'm not holding my breath about it anymore,
But a challenge.....I'm in the game for!!

January 1, 2012

Thursday, Friday and Saturday were beautiful days!
Perfect ending of a year in so many ways.
Tropic breezes, warmth, relaxing in the sun.
Sharing, caring, fishing and fun!
Wei barbecued fish, turkey wings and ribs;
Needless to say we'll have to wear bibs.
So Sunday to start the New Year,
Wei could watch the games and be clear

To relax and just enjoy the first day
Of 2012, which has come to stay!
Last night was New Years Eve
We sat on the deck, not wanting to leave.
See, here they do fireworks, like crazy to celebrate
The end of one year and the next ones coming fates
To both our east and west sides we watched,
Them shoot off fireworks, four hours on the clock.
From around seven till midnight or a little after
We watched the awesome show with laughter
Here we are, on the deck, with a glass of wine,
Bringing in the New Year, warm, and doing fine!!!

Monday, they are coming to do a short list
A different washing machine is my first wish.
Then a different yard light, with a new sensor;
So, it will stay on after dark, when Dad is out there.
Dad will also go get his coumadin check
And then go get fresh shrimp, to fish with...hi-tech!

Well we've come to the end of our first thirty days
We do miss you all...in so many ways!!
But, we're doing what we came here to do
Enjoying each other, the weather and of course FISHING TOO!!!

LOVE, Hugs, and Kisses to you all!! Miss You, but...we are liking it here, (right now.)

And we're still talking to each other!!!
MOM and DAD.....TOM and KAREN

Do let me know if you'd rather not hear about the next installment. (you should think about how I might not understand though, or how it might hurt my feelings, or how I could get upset 'cause nobody wants to hear or, or, ...). Never mind ......do let me know!!!!!!
Love Ya ALL!!!!!!!!!!!!!!

OUR RETIREMENT TRIP TO THE VALLEY 2
January 2012

Mornings are certainly quiet and peaceful here
My Tom is still sleeping till 10:00 it appears
This offers some quiet time to write, paint, read or do beading
Whatever I feel like, whichever I'm needing.
It is different from mornings I've known, that's true!
But, I have to admit I haven't a clue,
As to why, a sane person, would miss all the "hubbub" and such
(Shame on you, I know what you were thinking there)
When they are sitting here warm and not doing much?
Thinking about all that's going on back there
I face it! I miss all of that and I stare
Off in your direction and pass on my thoughts
So, that's why everyone of you sometimes get that knot.
You get the feeling, knowing, sensation,
That I'm watching you, so pay attention!
That's our "thing"; we're connected by our senses and feelings;
Not only related but, have binding thoughts and dealings!
Listen to them, feel them, and you will know,
I am there with you, always, wherever we all go!!!!!!!

IT is nippy this morning, 40 degrees.
Quit sending down that cold North breeze!
They brought a different washer to us yesterday

Don't know yet if this one will stay.
None of the washers are hooked to water that's hot,
And the gray water empties out on the lot!
The cardinals, mr. and mrs., are here this morning
Along with the squirrel that gives them the warning
When we open the door to throw out the goodies,
Because mr. squirrel likes the hydrox cookies!

Ech!, Saw my first cockroach today.
On the counter, he wanted to stay.
He did NOT get the chance to scurry away.
And will NOT be back on another day!!
They tell me that even in brand new houses,
They find these loathsome louses.
That's one of the things you deal with in Texas,
That's not a big price to pay for the good in the rest of it.
Gene and crew have come back to finish some stuff.
A couple odds and ends will be enough,
Making everything just right for us;
To live and play here and not make a fuss.
Tom is getting mighty restless.
Wants to go see what messes
We can get into hunting for live bait..
He's in a hurry and he can't wait!!
To Brownsville we're off to shop
For live bait, pipe tobacco, up I hop.?
We'll take the garmin, take us right there,
Except for gas pricing I wouldn't care.
Shopping is shopping, always, always fun.
Especially in no hurry and in the sun!
We have also made a name sign
Our names on it, his and mine.
It says Ritzers on it, as it should
Then we decided (this would be good);
To put on it Tom and His Wei.
Then under that put Karen for me.

We like it and we made it together
With wood and paint to withstand the weather.

It's now hanging out on the fence,
So, people will know where they have went!

Only a few more days, 4 to be exact
Till we know where internet can be at.
Now three days left till we get to see
If internet can come to you and me.
On the tenth they are scheduled
Let's hope for sure it is welded
Into their minds
To be on time!

January 7, 2012

Saturday was a delightful day
Just fishing, sunning and whiling away
But time to go in at four o'clock,
The games come on then, so we left the dock.
To watch the Saints and Texans win
And Sunday, the Giants and Broncos again.
Next weekend we think it's going to be
Green Bay of course, by maybe eight,
Also the Texans and the Saints
Dad thinks the Patriots (not the Texans) are going to win
I say the Broncos are a possible shoe - in.
We think the Forty-niners are going to make it.
And I agree to go with Dad and take it
Only time will tell who guessed right
By the end of next Sunday night.

January 10, 2012

THEY ARE HERE<THEY HAVE ARRIVED as I write,
The internet men have come to solve our plight.
They say we have to be in line of sight,
Of the tower; and they say we are alright!
They are busy hooking us up to the tower,
That will give us the use of internet power.
Will let you all know by an email
If you get it you'll be able to tell
WE GOT IT!!

January 11, 2012

Tonight the weather was good, stars out bright.
We both went fishing, turned on the dock light.
There came a green glow up in water.
Aliens come for a look??, No, twas your father
He turned on the underwater green light
That attracts the bait fish in at night.
So the bigger fish come in to feed
Then we can try to catch what we need
Dad is also going to try the casting net
To catch our own bait minnows, then we'll be set.
Catch our own bait, catch our own fish.
Then clean and cook, what more could we wish?
Just that we could all be down here doing this!!!

Tom got me the Barnes and Noble Nook tablet for my birthday
Without internet I couldn't get it started, no way!
So now my project is to get it up and running
For this to happen I will need cunning,
I'll have to figure it out by myself
No, others here to offer their expert help.
Up and going doing fine
Except when I go online.
They have me listed with my first Nook
Now I have to go in and have them look;

At what the problem is on their end
So I can surf on line and spend.

What a whirlwind weekend watching
All the teams that were botching
There chances of going to super bowl
Who could have guessed, who could know.
You could tell which teams wanted this so madly
By how the other teams played so badly!!!
Well on to the final weekend for the two games
Giants, Forty-niners, Ravens and Patriots are their names
I'm hoping for the Forty-niners and Patriots to win
Because their names sound like good old American.
Time will tell
I wish them well.

Got an e-mail from Sharon Holmen today
Jenny, Nick, Allan and Sharon are coming on Wednesday
To visit our place here in the sun,
It will be nice, it should be fun.
We went into town today
For a few things and to may
Be open a checking account here
So we don't have to have near
Every identification you can possibly think of
Just to get a coke or a bar of dove.
On our way home, Del called, said he could come by;
To show Tom how to give the casting net a try.
So we hurried on home, in very good time,
And Del came by to show dad so he could mime.
He tried his luck and really did okay
We told Del thank you, see you another day.
He told us Dolphins come down the river,
Early in the morning sunrise they shimmer.
You can see them playing out in the deep area
Now I'm going to have to get up earlier

To see if I can get a glimpse of these kings
For they are one of my most favorite of things.

The wei discovered she too could cast for bait
Now we no longer have to drive and wait
For the bait shops to get in their fresh fishes;
And Tom can have fresh bait when he wishes.
The wei caught at least twenty in that net,
It was warm enough out she didn't mind getting wet.
Some were pretty good size
So when Sam came by he was surprised (the Pelican)
That we could throw him a treat
But he would not come too close to eat
When he eats he's very neat.
He stretches out his beek and throat,
And after he swallows does not gloat!

Wednesday, today January 18, twenty twelve
We are going to have visitors to delve
Into talk about life here in the valley
Coming to see how they will tally
Our place here in Arroyo Cove
And how long it was they drove
To find us out here and what they think;
The house and yard are ready and in the pink.
We had a nice time visiting and catching up
Watching the barges and wild animals and such.
They told us about the citrus parade on the 28th
If you want a good view you can't be late.
Also all Dickinson county peoples dinner out
Is Feb. 2nd, we'll all be there no doubt.
It's going to be at Mr. Getty's restraunt
So everyone can have just what they want.
We'll get to see all the other folks
From back home and make a toast,
To all you back home in the snow and cold.

A toast to you all, for we are not as bold;
And came here to have a warm get-a-way
Spending time outside in the sun most every day.

Tomorrow we go to Mexico for lunch;
And some shopping I have a hunch!!
Probably a margaritta or two
Depending on whose driving who!!!
Oh well there goes that....
For I do wish to make it back!!!!
While there we'll get some new movie releases
This time around, some good pieces.
Of some glassware I saw last time
Their cost is minimal only, dimes
We also got some perfumes that smell
Wonderful, and Dad can tell
When I have on Jennifer Anniston's
Instead of some of the other ones.
  He got another bottle of Perry Ellis's   (he's used up the bottle
                                                he got from Tina)
Because of comments about it from the waitresses.
Picked up some fresh veggies and fruit
While on the way home, we did scoot.
So we could get home to fish and get bait
Before it got to dark and to late.
Well that's it for this week, they're going by way to fast.
Before we know it, it will be our last.
So sending this off via e-mail this time
Now that we have internet...the paper can be on your dime.
You guys print it off...read or throw away.
Cause I'll be writing more on another day

Love MOM   January 20, 2012

OUR RETIREMENT TRIP TO THE VALLEY 3
JANUARY 20, 2012

Friday night the neighborhood started to grow
Neighbors everywhere, both sides of us, did show
Up to enjoy this unseasonably good winter weather
The day on Saturday was perfect, couldn't be better.
We met the Garzas to our East
Both brothers and their wives had a feast
On their dock, while they looked.
Your dad had a tarpon on his hook.
It is true! But, it shook itself loose
After several spectacular leaps and boosts
Then to our west, Mr. Yates came in
With his brother and dog, to go for a spin
Out to catch some fish in the bay,
They didn't come back till later in the day.
Two doors farther down to the west,
Several families came together to nest
For the weekend with the whole tribe
Swimming, fishing, music and boat rides.
It was like our lakes back home in season
Just a beautiful day for everyone to enjoy, for no particular reason.
It reminded me of home so much;
I missed being back there, AM I TOUCHED??

I asked myself... Do I remember the cold and snow?
YES I DO!...So I let that thought go!
We had barbecued chicken tonight on the grill
Oh yes, Dad wants his chicken still!!
After we ate we went back down to the dock
As was everyone else up and down the block.
We could have read a book out there
There was so much light from everywhere.
Everyone out trying for that big fish
I hope some of them get that wish.
As for me, I'm going up to head
For a movie and the couch instead.
Till Tom has had enough fishin' for this day,
And decides to come in for poker play.
Until he tires or takes his meds;
Then for him too, it's off to bed.
Sunday the wind is haulin' a--lot
Dad woke up and thought, oh not!
I guess I'll wait till the wind dies down
So read the paper and had breakfast with a frown.
He finally decided to go down and check the line
He had left out all night, it was doing fine.
Fished awhile, then threw it out;
Came back in to watch the bouts
Between the 49ers and Giants, Ravens and Patriots
Finding out who would make the cuts
So Giants and Patriots will battle for the title
Of Super bowl Champs, and more kids to idol,
The players and teams,
American male dreams!
Monday brings clouds and overcast;
Looks like it could rain at last.

That's ok, we've lots to do.
Like writing this down to all of you.

We caught a pelican on our line,
More like he swam into it, BUT HE'S DOING FINE!
We didn't panic, but reeled him in,
Then the real fun did begin.
Cut him loose, and unwound the sinker.
Off he went...will he be a thinker?
About getting friendly and in too close;
Not everyone would have got him loose.
Some would have said, cut the line,
He'll be fine!
We'd rather help him be free
So he will not be afraid of me.   (us really but it didn't rhyme)

Painting has become a chore
Even if it's something I adore.
If I paint inside and get paint on the floor
It isn't actually ours to mess or do more.
But, if I go outside to paint
It's like the farm; never wind. There AIN'T!!
Then the canvas blows too
And bugs stick on the new
Oh my! Not being able to paint every day, OH DRAT!!
So, isn't it a shame I have to contend with that!!!
And the other things we have to put up with here;
Sun, watching the wildlife, fishing, relaxing and then a mere
70 degrees or more almost every day
And this is their winter they say!

Mail man came by today to deliver.
A package from home to us down by the river.
He brings it up in the yard and honks his horn,
We come out and take the mail, after the morn.
Is over...usually around twelve-thirty.
We say thank you, and he says, "just doing my duty"
He really says, "no problem, Mam"

And we go in and open it as fast as we can.
Dad loves getting the paper from back there,
Staying in touch with the nosey side of his care
About what's going on and whose doing what,
To whom and why and how for how much.
So now he's got his papers for the week
And I'll not see his nose unless he peeks
Out to say, could I have more coffee, please?
And of course, I say get it for yourself and sneeze   (ya sure)
While I say it, and go get it anyway!!
I haven't trained him differently yet, on our stay.
But, I'm working on it,
Trying to change the habit!

A Brownsville trip was on the agenda for today
A stop at the post office, and walmart on the way
On to Sams Club and the Cigar store
For a lighter that stays lit in the wind and more.
Sams club was an interesting stop
Five gallon pails of dill pickles and other things top
A long list of what was so very unique
Like six pounds of string cheese coiled in a heap.
It reminded us of a California trip we all once took,
Where string cheese was hung like ropes from a hook.
We found, we hope, a good kind of wine.
Tried it and tasted better than fine.
It's name is Moscato D'Asti from Italy,
In a pretty blue bottle that first got to me.
The sign said slightly sweet, slightly sparkling
I like it, now seeing if we can get it at home is the thing.
I'm reading all the fine print on the bottle
It's imported by Prestige Wine Group, Princeton, Mn.
What a coincidence, like while we've been in Texas,
All we hear on TV is about Iowa and the caucuses.
Like the young man in the Cricket internet store

Spent two years in Omaha and been to the Lakes for...
A weekend with some other friends
Coincidences abound, there's no end.
We're on our way home, and on the car thermometer;
91*, no wonder Dad wants on the air conditioner.
But this morning was funny, Waking up we were both cold!
50* difference since yesterdays heat so bold!
They say this is an unusually warm winter here,
Just like you guys are having up there.

Friday, calm, sunny, fishing, b-b-queing.
We actually saw a Nilgai for one and a half hours of viewing
Got lots of pictures to see how he moves
He probably weighed in at 800 pounds, but can't prove
But we could see how he blends in with the bush
We were watching him graze and still needed to push
Our eyes into focus to see him
He does that good a job of blending in
They were originally brought here in the thirties.
To the King ranch with other rare birdies
They got away and have flourished in the wild
I can't wait to see a mommy with a child.

We went to watch the Citrus Parade on Saturday.
Sharon and Allan Holmen showed us the way.
Their park had a float in the parade
It got first place the one they all made
The theme this year was based on Marde Gras
They had dignataries, floats, cars, and princesses
Veterans and horses, plus people to clean up messes.
It was a great parade, two and a half hours long
Food and balloons, tumblers, and bands with songs.

We said thank you, and see you in a few days
At the Dickinson County gathering at Mr. Gattys.

Rain, rain, rain, wonderful rain.
Came down hard and stopped our phone again.
But it came back on later in the day
Stopped raining so Tom could go down to the bay,
To fish, and me, I went down to throw the casting net
Got him about twenty of the little fish so wet.
That he uses for bait,
To change the bigger fishes fate.
Got some washing done and juiced some fruit
Sent off some mail, and did commute,
Out to the mail box, on the highway
It's only about a block and a half away.
About the same as going to ours back home
Except no snow, so don't need to take the phone.
Finishing our taxes is next on my list
Get them sent off for 2011; it's just!
I wish we could just send them our money,
And not do the figures to show why; now that would be funny!

King has made the Texas room his domain
When we can't locate him it's always the same
He's out there, up on the back of the couch
So he can scan each direction and look out
Without getting up and using to much energy
To keep track of us and the animals he can see.

Well the end of another thirty days   January 30, 2012
Soon it will be the end of our stay.
You all take care, stay healthy and safe
Soon we will get to see your smiling face.
Miss you all a lot, we love you too!!
Stay out of trouble and do what you need to do!!!

Love: Mom and Dad; Grandpa and Grandma; Tom and Karen

Retirement Trip To The Valley 4
February 2nd 2012

Went to McAllen across the Rio Grande Valley
To see everyone from Dickinson County, so we could tally;
How many we know and how many we didn't
There were quite a few, that's why we all went.
Had some pizza and salad like our Pizza Ranch
Then followed Allan and Sharon Holmen, got a great chance,
To see a glass cutter and design maker, Knew at a glance,
Sharon and Allan will learn a lot about stained glass
If they follow his guidance and take his class.
See, that's their hobby, it's what they do together
They cut and lead in patterns in glass, whether
It be an apple or a lighthouse on the rocks,
To guide sailors into their docks.....
They already really do beautiful things
I'm anxious to see what the years will bring!
Got to see Jenny and Nic Vos
Jenny organized the event she was the Boss.
Nic helped her too, their anniversary was two days ago
Donna and Dick Christoffer were there also.
They were so nice to save us a spot
A lot of others mightin' have not.
One of their children is coming with family for a visit
We told them to bring them out, see what's all in it.

The river area, where we are existing,
When we're here, and the cold we're missin'???   (not this
                                                          year huh!)

This afternoon there was some commotion behind us
Looked out to see what was causing the fuss.
WOW!!! Is all I can say.
Because of what we saw today!
An alligator at least seven foot, tail to head
Was sunbathing on the dock.; I thought it was dead!!
The Garzas spotted it in the dog leg, they're from our east
They say they see them on their lawn at least
Once or twice or more every year
You see them sunbathing over here.
They don't bother anyone though,
They're more afraid of you, You know.!
Then a man from the mobile park, a few blocks up
Came by and said hello, chatted, what's up.
He was born in Iowa, Waterloo
Knew of the lakes, a thing or two.
Has stayed in Florida, and now lives in Missouri
But, comes south when it starts to flurry.
He got to see the gator also,
That shiny seven foot long torso,
Laying on the old dock ..stretched out sleeping
I'm glad he's not prone to coming around creeping.

It's supposed to rain this weekend
So, I'll be starting my taxes then
And work on them Sunday while watching this big Game.
I hope the Giants get to win, if it's all the same
To all of you; cause I like them better then the other team
If the Giants don't win, I'll probably scream.

Saturday afternoon, I'm trying to work on the taxes

Listening to the thunder, watching through the glasses
Seeing it darken with the black clouds rolling in,
It's raining cats and dogs, creating quite a din
The temperature has dropped thirty degrees
No wonder I feel as though I could freeze.
Dad's out on the porch
Playing on line poker of course.
He even asked for a jacket
I heard him above the racket.
He got chilly outside on the porch,
So I got him his four o'clock pills and a torch   (not really, it
                                                              rhymed)

I got him his jacket, and opened up the house
To let the fresh air in while he's off the couch.
We noticed Sam the pelican standing on the dock in the rain.
He was bathing away that's probably why he came,
Our dock has no canopy or wooden cover
So he could stand and preen and not have to hover,
On a post precariously perched
To do his special hygiene work.

The super bowl came and went,
Liked the commercials and Clint   (Eastwoods message I liked)
Giants won, not a surprise
They played better than the other guys.

Today, Sam came by to visit with Dad,   (the pelican)
Of course he wanted some fish, he thought Dad had.
They visited quite awhile, and watched each other
Dad fed him the fish, and then called on Mother;
To come down to the dock to cast net some more.
Sam was still hungry, but no fish came to shore.
I took some pics, went back up to do some more things
Dad stopped fishing. Sam took to his wings....
Another busy day, relaxing and visiting

And, oh, can't forget fishing, while it was misting.

New movie releases come out on Tuesday
Probably go to Mexico to get them on Thursday
They are getting better at this knock of stuff
I can see why the industry is in a huff
They cost us three dollars apiece
For those new movies just released..
Sometimes their quality is not the best
But then we get to watch them at rest,
At home, at our own pace
Not have to drive anywhere or line up in the race.
Taxes are done, sending them off today
Will mail them on our merry way,
To Mexico to get more margaritas and new movies,
Listen to serius radio; the channels that are "groovy"

Also mailing some things off for Valentines Day,
It's just a note, to let us just say
We love our kids, grandchildren, relatives and friends,
And in about six weeks we'll be home again.
The time has gone fast, but don't despair!
We'll be back soon, to be "in your hair!!"
We'll not be bringing back very much for souvineers.
Spent a bit on just being able to be here
Only kidding, we'll think of something I'm sure.
But, probably not something that will endure,
As long as our memories of one another.
So, always pay attention to your Mother!
Life can be what you want it to.
If you work hard and apply yourself to do!;
What it takes to get the task done,
Whether it's money, work, happiness, love or fun.
The keys are; mind set, work, and follow through.
And one other thing to your own heart be true.

Enough of thoughts from me. I'm OLD!
Sometimes you have to learn for yourself, I'm told!!!

WE got a chess set the smallest one they had.
When Mr. Christoffer comes to play chess with Dad.
While Donna and their son go fishing in the bay,
He'll come here to spend time while they're away.

I just got back, from three hours off on my own.
Dad insisted he stay home.
I was going to call him to say "Honey I miss you!"
I know what he would say, "long distance, Don't Do!"
So, when I got back, I told him about it.
Sure enough he said, "I would have thrown a fit."
I was gone because of a new bottle of flax seed;
It had been opened, and to return it, was the need.
We never know anymore, about peoples causes.
So, back it went without any pauses.

Dick called and he'd been at the Riders   (IN Arkansas)   Feb 10,
                                                                                      2112

Tomorrow morning he'll be a flighter
And come south to see us way down here,
He thinks Sunday sometime he will appear.
It's about 800 miles from Dallas to Harlingen
Lots and lots of miles from where he's been.
He actually arrived Saturday evening.
Made excellent time from where he was leaving.
He found Rio Hondo and drove right to us
Didn't involve much of a fuss.
Sunday we showed him a few of the sights close by
But it had to rain, no sun in the sky.

We got some fresh bait for fishing
The weather could be better we were wishing

He saw where the alligator had been
And where the pelicans come up to him.
Our yard, and trees and flowers and much
More, inside the house and all the stuff, such

As where the river bends and turns
Birds and wildlife and cactus and ferns.
Tonight we'll take him to the restraunt here
We'll have Mexican cuisine, a mere.
Less than a mile from our place;
With a wharf, wile we dine the river we'll face.
Change of plans, fish were biting but, we're running out of fresh bait
So back to the bait shop and the Mrs. there made us dinner late.
Back to the dock,
Fish till 10:00.

Monday it still looked overcast
But the sun came out at last.
We went into town
To show Dick around
And to eat at the Crazy China Buffet
Tom and Dick, fished and probably wanted to stay
But, we went into town anyway!
We had a little interesting sight tonight
As Dick and Dad fished in the light
A Dolphin Pod came by,
One breeching the water up high,
Ten foot long was the guys guess,
I got down there to see them just,
As they moved on farther down stream
Looking for more fish is their dream.
They did not come back up the river
While I was down there watching hither
But we're glad Dick got to see them too

Otherwise everyone wouldn't have believed us, Would You?
The guys have so many fish in their baskets
They're complaining and think they have to ask
Does anyone around here clean fish?
And no one does, But, they can wish!

HAPPY VALENTINES DAY, the sun is out.
The guys are down cleaning fish with pouts
The doors and windows are open to let in fresh air
And I can here their banter down there
They had all kinds of the guy neighbors come visit
On the dock, they all sat and "kibitzed"
I'm going down later to take some pictures
We'll see if the pelicans remain permanent fixtures.
We saw some deer across the Arroyo
A beautiful buck, with a very large rack and his doe

Mr. Betey came to dig in a conduit line
Across the yard so all will be fine.
We had a small problem with a breaker trippin'
Whenever it rained it started flippin'
Then we couldn't use the microwave
Except on a drop cord plugged in across the way
We had catfish nuggets and sea trout for supper
And then the guys went back down to "suffer"
Fishing again, do they ever get enough?
Evidently not enough of that stuff!!!

The Orange, lemon, and lime trees are in bloom
The aroma is fantastic in every room.
Dick is preparing to leave today
By 10:00 he wanted to be on his way.
BUT, he left a little later;
Because we spied the Gator
He's bigger than we first thought

Ten foot long and 30″ across.   (guessing of course because we
                                      didn't go measure)
So we got to see the gator neighbor before he left to roam,
We got some pictures, and off he went on his way home.
Wouldn't you know it, before he left we discussed one of the things
he missed seeing;
An hour after he left it came into being,
Down the Arroyo came the barge;
It was loaded down and quite large.
So, Dad called him to tell him, YUP, you just missed it!
Otherwise he saw all our little get-a-way place has to offer with
Smells and sights
And fishing delights!!!!!

We've also found out that the plant operation across the street
Is a farm of sorts and grows something to eat!
It's a fresh shrimp farm operation
That's probably why the gator hangs in his location.
They get their brackish water from his lagoon
And recirculate it back there, and he gets to eat at noon.
So on goes the adventure in Texas,
Come down, visit, have breakfast!!!!
Love Mom and Dad

Our Retirement Trip 4-2
February 17th 2012

It's rainy today and over cast
But still seventy degrees and at last,
I can get the bunk house ready
In case we have some company, steady.
Mr. Gilliam, call me Robert, he says,
To invite us at noon tomorrow for fish.
Just a few of us locals getting together
We have a big porch, don't worry about weather.
Well, we got to go and meet everyone
Have to admit they were all fun.
His wife's name is Janice,
She is very nice and humorous.
Gerald is one of their sons that was there
With his wife Yoli, she has beautiful dark hair.
Del was there also, and Rosa and Joe
And the couple that hasn't been around for a year or so.
Gerald and Yoli, Robert and Janice,
Are going on a week cruise tomorrow, Yoli is Spanish.
Their poodles, Bubba, Sugar and Beau
Are going to stay with Rosa and Joe.
Everyone was from this Arroyo Cove Rd.
It's nice to know you, we've been told.

So, they are all a good bunch of neighbors
Making it nice to be here and in our favor.

February 20, 2012

Monday we went in for the coumadin check;
And on into town, ah what the heck.
Tom, got a five dollar hair buzz
And then we're going to eat here because,
Each time we come in for this
We try a new place and a new dish.
We had leftovers, enough
For lunch tomorrow, that will be rough.
Also got vitamins at Walgreens, buy one get one free.
Got some nuts, and some sugarless candy.
Filled up the gas tank before heading home
Filled up the seven water jugs we own.

The bunk house is all ready to go
Now, anyone can show up with kids in tow.
Cleaned out the inside of the van
Did the best the wei can
Without a power washer to scrub the floors
Wiped down everything, including the doors
Planted some petunias around the yard.
To add some color, the ground isn't hard.
It's mostly compiled of shells, and dirt and sand
Pretty sure this is recaptured land.
When they built the sea wall along the Arroyo,
To prevent erosion and silting, you know!

I'm going to check with some nurseries
To see if they have some pomegranate trees.
I'd love to have one growing here
Maybe we'll have some next year.

I'm actually sitting out on the porch
Thinking I need more citranella for the tiki torch,
Next time we go into town.
That's why I make a list, and write it down.

Today the air is still, no breeze.   Feb 21, 2012
First time in a while, no wind, I'm pleased.
I can paint today.
My canvas won't blow away!
While I'm on the deck painting,
I can smell the orange blossoms, faintly.
On the still air
Looking at the river I stare.
What part do I want to put on this canvas
It is so peaceful, the river, wild life, this has it
All, so I have to pick which scene.
Do I want it surreal or pristine?

Two more days and Jon Jon will be here
With his family he holds dear.
They're driving down thru Oklahoma City
To see some sights and country pretty.
Then to Dallas, to the famous spot,
Where Kennedy's fate was made with a shot.
While in Texas, also see the Alamo
Where they fought and lost, you know!
Then down to us to spend some time
Relaxing, playing, fishing and kind
Of getting the feel of Texas retirement
Before going back to all the excitement.

They arrived in the early morning hours,
Technically the 25th, we turned on all the power.
So they could find us in the dark,
And start the fun and visit parks.

Saturday was rainy, so we went to South padre
To see the Gulf and go to Market Days.
Tom and Jon signed up for a Gulf fishing trip
To figure they would do that did not take a lot of wit.
The pirate ship tour was the choice for the rest of us,
With sword fighting, cannon bursts and tough
Pirates; Aye, Aye matey was their call
And we get to see Dolphins, we're on the Gulf after all.
Sunday we went to Mexico, across the border.
Boys all got their hair cuts, made to order.

Jade got a wrap braid put in her hair.
Joseph did it, but Pedro was also there.
Jonathan was a big hit with the Mexicans,
They thought he was a giant among men.
We had lunch there, Mexican Cuisine;
Upstairs at the Red Snappers mezzanine.
Marge and Jon got some pills,
And a few other little frills.
We came back through customs without a hitch,
With identification and birth certificates.
Monday they went shopping at the Outlet Mall
Got some large size shoes for Jon and Jonathon, because they're
so tall.
All the people in the store thought it was amazing
They couldn't believe somebody needed that size, it was dazing!!
Ethan and Jade and Marge had fun,
Looking and watching while on the run.
Fishing nightly for all has been the case.
Jonathan can throw the casting net with grace,
Jade and Marge are catching crabs in the net;
Also little ghost shrimp in the trap they get.
Ethan likes feeding the pelicans and gulls.
They fly overhead and catch the fish, they never get full.

We all went to Brownsville and Boca Chica Beach
Played in the waves, that seemed like we'd never reach.
Miles and miles of coast line bays
Picked up some shrimp, from the seafood market
Went back home, cooked them and liked it.
Tonight Jonathon cast the net and caught a Tarpon,   24" long)

Feb 29th 2012

Some bait fish and several other kinds to keep the guys from harpin'
Marge and Jade caught a good blue crab
Ethan ran back and forth and knows how to gab!!
Tom and Jon caught trout and other fish
Telling each other all along, a lot of bull_ _ _ _.
Thursday back to South Padre Island we went
After seeing Bobz World Museum, and hour spent.
Went to Pier 19 to eat
Shrimp and Grouper with Gulf view seats.
Sent the Guys off for bay fishing
As for the rest of us we are wishing
To do some shopping, got some Boogie Boards
And off to ride the waves, putting on the wrist cords.
Jade and Jonathon got the hang of it.
Marge and Ethan liked the sand castle bit.
Some people were flying kites
Some people were on walking hikes.
Then off we went to pick up the guys
Fishing was done and we heard the "whys"
The fish were cleaned right on the spot,
And Ethan, Jade, Jonathon and Jon got
To feed the gulls and pelicans,
And off we went to home again.
Our final night before they have to depart,
Jonathan cast the net and for a start,

Caught a Mullet Grouper a pretty good lot
Besides the bait fish he always got.
Jade was a trooper, the brave heart.

Got in the river water in the dark
To get the cast net untangled
From a pier post it dangled.
She did what the guys didn't want to;
Our hats off to her, a brave soul, TRUE BLUE!
Marge, Ethan, Jade and I watched
The Twilight, New Dawn movie we bought
In Mexico for three dollars a shot.
Morning brought the time for departure
A little remorse going on for sure.
Sorry to leave, sorry to see them go,
But glad they came to visit us on the Texas Arroyo!!!!!!!!!!!!

Our Retirement Trip To The Valley 6...Final Chapter

March 17th

Happy St. Patrick's Day
I wore green today.
Nobody but me and your Dad to see it tho'
I could have gone naked nobody would know!....NOT!!!
There are some college kids two doors down
For Spring Break they came to town.
Garzas to the east were here for the weekend
Gene to the west came by to visit and then tend
To a group at her house of fishermen.
They caught 17 trout
In their one night bout.   (off her dock)
Dad took apart the scooter carts
Neither seemed to have working parts
He cleaned and pushed connections
Checked batteries and directions
And by gosh, got the job done!
He got them both to now run.

March 18th

Today we sat on the dock.........(They call it a pier here)
Fishing, talking, not watching the clock!
Oh my gosh, he's got a big one
Thought he was in for some good fun.

Turned out to be a big tree branch
For a moment or two we thought by chance
A big fish!, No such luck!
Pulling it in really sucked!
Got that done and out of the water
Threw out again, waited a bit as it got hotter.
Low and behold another good bite.
But this time for real..it was agood fight!
I got the net, while Tom fought
We landed a 30″ long spotted trout!
Took a picture for proof, and filleted it out!

Our Retirement trip to the Valley
6 final chapter part 2
March 18th

We also caught a sea gull in flight.
Got him loose, let him go without to much fright.
I was bar b queing chicken for supper
Lo and behold looked up at 'er.
Mr. gator neighbor was back on HIS dock.
Watching the birds land and flock
Into the trees right above him.
Stayed there several hours, drying his skin.
Then while we were eating out on the deck
He slipped in the water, could just see his head and neck.
He floated over right under the birds
None of them moved or said a word!
He laid there awhile, tail barely moving
Keeping him in place like a boat at it's mooring.
At dusk he meandered over to his nest.
I suppose to get a good nights rest.
Dad went back fishing
Another big one he was wishing!
He called me on the two way radio.
Down to the dock (pier) I did go.
The cart had stopped working...
So wei pushed it to where the raccoon was lurking.
We loaded it into the van

In the morning it's going to the repairman.
After we dropped it off
We made another stop..............(At Sam's Club)
Dad got some baggy shorts
The kind kids wear for summer sports
Also got the kids a surprise
Can't wait to see their eyes!
Tuesday the van is being serviced and made ready
To drive home to Iowa sure and steady.
But first one more trip to Mexico
And pack a day or two, then we'll go
But that's not for two weeks yet
So, I still have time not to fret.
Dad asked me when does the van go in?
I answered in the morning before ten.
He said oh, go on, don't wake me!
So, he'll stay here and I'll go see.
Have the service and everything checked,
Be back before he gets in his total rest!
Coffees ready, phone is by his head;
Off I go to get this done, I don't dread.
I'll take my Nook
Enjoy my book!
While I wait
Piece of cake!!
I was home before Eleven
Look who is up watching CNN!
Walked in the door, the phone rang,
It had rained, can't hear a thing, DANG!
Have to go outside and use the cell,
It was Ruebin, trying to tell..........................(no, not Rob, the repairmans real name)

Us, the cart is fixed, and we can pick up at will,
So, off we went to Brownsville.
So, guess how much it did cost to fix it.

Nope!..Twenty-five dollars was all, plus I gave him a tip.
We tried a new way down and a different way back.
Much quicker, less miles, and more to look at!
The rained stopped before noon.
The wind dispersed the gloom
Of the dark clouds, the sun came out
Another nice day to play about!

March 21st

Dad is fishing again today,
But I asked him to take Helen some supper down the way.
He also is taking some to Janice and Robert
Swiss steak it is, I'm clearing out cupboards.
That only took him two hours and a half.
The "guys" started yakking, I had to laugh!!
They say women are the ones who gossip;
I know differently, because I've watched it!
Well, we've learned that this year the shrimp hatchery
Across the way, is not growing shrimp they say;
But, Talapia, for the stores around the area
So they can buy and sell and not need a carrier,
To distribute and keep iced and such
And to the customers shouldn't cost as much.
Tonight is a beautiful evening
Even though the temperature was heating,
At five o'clock p.m.
It read one hundred and ten,
Took a picture of it!
I, quite frankly am loving it!
Dad went down to fish in the breeze
The man next door (Gregg) was mowing and sneezed.
He's going to stay awhile and fish later.
He asked, if we'd seen the gator?
Not in a day or two
We'll let you know if we do.
Gregg went up to get his gear,
And Dad got a big one on, GET THE NET DEAR!

This one he had to play for awhile.
It was a Tarpon, quite a trial!
Measured in at 31" long
Shinny white and very strong.
He also caught more sea trout
Which is what his fishing is about.
While I was sitting with him, radio playing
Reading my Nook and looking at stars displaying.
I looked down and saw a darkness
Mass moving next to my feet.
Freaked me out; but, I got to meet
Rocky raccoon, out to eat
The fish and shrimp Dad had thrown on the dock.
He ran, I jumped, and your father mocked.
I said, I've had enough for tonight!
I went up to turn on the outside lights.
So, your father could see to park his cart
And come inside, not in the dark!

March 22

This morning I went out
To feed the birds and hear them shout
Out to each other, time to eat
We can all come out now and get our treats.
The rabbit, the squirrels and the birds.
Seem to talk to each other and spread the word.
I grabbed my coffee and sat on the deck,
Watching them communicate and what the heck?;
Some seagulls came to eat the crackers.
Blackbirds and gracklings didn't like their laughter.
Chased the seagulls away, biting at their tail ends.
But the seagulls came back with lots more of their friends!
They ate the stale crackers and then left.
Then the woodpecker came in to join the rift.
It began again between them and the red wings
Even the green jay had to fight for a few things.
The squirrels ate the peanuts,

Rabbit's a few of the carrot cuts.
A large barge came by as I sipped on my coffee
ANNNND< I SWEAR JUST NOW I GOT TO SEE!
The Dolphin Pod go by, free as can be.!
Doing the arc thing in the Arroyo
Like they knew I was watching you know!
Of course I did not have my camera out there with me,
And if I go in to get it I'll miss them see?
But, the sighting of them made me very happy!!!!

March 23rd

Helen came by today
Came with her walker up this way.
She stayed and chatted for an hour or two.
Saying several times, "Won't you stay? I'll miss you guys",
We have to answer nay, we have family ties'
We want to get back to see our friends and Family!!
For they mean a lot to us, you see.
She surprised me saying she thought I was around thirty-eight
All my children are older than that for goodness sake.!!......(Just had to remind you all how old you are)
But it made me feel a little better about myself
Not quite so much like an overgrown elf.
We found out her true age.
But she swore us to secrecy, that's a whole 'nother page!!
She tells everyone she's over sixty-five
Can collect social security and that's no lie
But she does not want the others along here to know her true count!
Then they'd get all mushy, and problems would mount.
They'd start stopping by to see how she's doing
She wouldn't be able to nap without shooing,
Them away and stuff like that,
So, we honor her wishes, that's a fact!!
March 26...the countdown begins
And truthfully we're ready now for it to end............(for this season)
One week left to organize and pack

I wish we could close the door, and start back.
But, it's time to make some calls.
Cancel this and that 'till fall.

AT&T, to put phone on vacation,
Call about box pick-up and destinations.
The store asked to bring your packages to us,
And we'll get them sent out via UPS
We're going to leave the trailer behind,
Parked at Maddie and Greggs double -wide
Garage, more like a huge Quonset hut
And we'll have more room for the putts   (cat)
We won't be bringing near as much next year
Now we know what we use and don't, here.
Next year I'll probably leave the beads.
Just take the paints and writing needs.
Change of plans, Maddie called and said,
You can leave the trailer right there in the shed.
So, we can just pack it instead.

March 29,

Went to take more packages to ship...
Before we went over to Mexico one last trip.
On the way Dad wanted one last Churches Chicken
Big mistake on my part, I had a bone sticken'
Coughed and choked, guess I finally spit it out!
Luckily I wasn't driving when I had the 'bout.
So, all turned out well, and off we went.
Our last excursion into Margaritta time, well spent.
Picked up some meds, and a batch of movies,
And got a spray painted picture for Pam, no duties!
On our way back filled up the gas tank.
And what a shock to be quite frank!!
All that's left is to pack and leave!

March 30th

Mr. Gator Neighbor popped in to say good bye.
Tom saw him first, then so did I.

We got to say good-bye to him 'till next year.
Wait a minute what did I just hear!!!!!!!!!!!!!!!
Yup, it was just what I feared,
Dad, rolled the cart out back
He did it so he wouldn't have to help pack.   (not really)
I had to go help him get up and untangled
Get the legs back straight and the cart finnagled.
After that, darned if he didn't bang his head
On the open door trailers edge.
Now he's going to look abused!!
And beat upon, That's my excuse!!!
All done for today!!
Now supper, then stay,
On the couch for the rest of the evening
Tomorrow, the van packed and then will be leaving.

Got up started dismantling things   April 2, 2012
Packing tightly in the van begins
Took all day, we got it done, went to bed
Monday morning bright and early,
Head North in a little hurry!!
Now getting anxious to see everyone!!
Especially the Family and have some fun.
At seven-thirty a.m. we took off.

At one o'clock in Austin we did stop
To meet Evonne and Tom Smith at Lake Austin
We got to see their new home...AWESOME!!!!!
White Oak beams from a hundred year old barn   (was in
                                                        Pennsylvania)
Walnut floors upstairs from an old Tabacco farm   (was in
                                                        Tennessee)
From near by quarries, Hand chiseled White limestone
Wrought iron railings from Blacksmiths, hand honed.
The first thought that comes to mind,
It is definitely going to be one of a kind!!!

Now on to see Delores and Gary in Dallas
Then the rest of the way home we <u>galloped</u> (Remember we were
still in Texas)

Had a very nice visit,
Their home is exquisite.
Made it home on Tuesday around noon,
And not really any to soon,
Dallas area got tornadoes and bad weather
Right after we went through their hills of heather.
Topeka had rain while Tom was behind the wheel
While I was driving, always on an even keel!   (not according
to Tom)

Good to be home at last!!
And really not tooooo fast.
Good to see everyone again.............
Now our first retirement story ends!

Hope you all enjoyed our little story,
And it kept you informed, but wasn't to borey.

Love, Mom and Dad...Tom and Karen
Home Again
THE END!!

TWO OF
MY OWN POEMS
DON'T GRIEVE FOR ME
WHEN I AM GONE
AND
JUST A WARNING

Don't Grieve For Me
When I Am Gone
(put in the paper, and use if
there is a service when I go.)

Listen To My Last Words For You!

Don't grieve for me when I am not physically here
For I am with you, always near
Don't cry or grieve, or even weep
For I am alive in the memories you keep.
In all the things we've done,
Places we've been, songs we've sung.
And all the times we were together
Whether it was stormy or nice weather.
For if you remember even a part;
Then I live on in your Hearts!

If you have memories of me, good or bad,
Then celebrate!! Don't be sad.
If we've had some spats
Don't be sorry for that.
For if you truly have memories,
I will remain in your hearts and heads
And will only be in body, Dead.

If I have lived a life very long
Think about me with a song;
And even if my life was short
Don't grieve for me when I am gone.
For if you remember then I live on!

Remember things we did and shared.
Things we cherished, things we dared,
Remember please, The laughs, the tears,
Times remembered thru' the years.
For together we did feel,
Whether it be fond or not,
It just means I was real.
Real in thoughts and real in deeds
And hopefully filled someones needs.
Of those around me, far and close.

So pick-up your glasses, I propose a Toast!!
To all the memories of all my life,
Glad to be my husbands wife.
Happy to be my children's Mother.
And fond of knowing all you others!!
You all contribute to my memories,
For without all of you, I wouldn't be;
The person I want you to remember, **ME!!!**

When I GO continued.....

So, Don't grieve for me, just remember,
And I will live with you all, forever.

I leave you all in body only
Always near, so you won't be lonely.
Think of me, when I am gone,
And I will live, on and on.

If you do all these things
I shall still live among you;
If you do not.
Then I will be forgot!!

SMILE FOR ME! Have memories, laugh, and rejoice
For you know now that would be, for all of you, my choice.
So, Bye for now, 'Till we meet Again.
But not, by any means, the end!
Take care of each other, for I am watching, I AM!
Love to you all!
Your, Conspirator, Wife, Mother and Friend.

IN MY LIFE, I have lived, I have loved, I have lost, I have missed,
I have hurt, I have trusted
I have made mistakes, I have made friends, and I have probably
made enemies.....
But most of all, I HAVE LEARNED...............unknown author

A special Thank You to my Mother, Wanda and Father, Bob Taylor
and sister, Barbara; For helping me so much on my path to "grown
up". (some may say I never got there).
And to my husband of 56 years, Thank you, Tom, for all those years
we had together.
And my Special Thanks to my Children, Rob, Tina and Teresa for
raising Mom in the past several years. You are my treasures, along
with my Grandchildren, Nicholas and Cynthia. During this life and
beyond, forever..........Karen Rae (Taylor) Ritzer

Poems For: When I'm Gone from This Life

#1
Just a Warning

When I go, I'll be in the clouds
Watch for me there
I'll be riding a Unicorn
Or lounging with puppies
Or climbing a mountain,
Riding a train.
Picking some flowers
Playing with children,
Visiting a different world.
But, If you look for things in the clouds
I' will be there, watching over you all!

Behave yourselves! For if you don't,
I'll bring Lightning and Thunder down
To show my disappointment!
If you are unhappy, hurting, or ill,
I'll rain or snow down tears for you.
And if the world is showing nothing but ill will,
Their will be disasters to destroy and chill.

Whatever happens,
I will be with you all.
In your memories, and in the clouds.
Watch for me up there!
And on the clearest of nights
Look up to the stars,
And know I am with you,
Wherever you are!!

Karen Rae (Taylor) Ritzer

BIOGRAPHY
FOR
KAREN RAE
(TAYLOR) RITZER

Karen Rae (Taylor) Ritzer Bio

World War II Ended on December 2, 1945. My Dad, Robert L. Taylor from Sioux City, Iowa, came home from the European Theater; where he ran radio wires ahead into enemy lines for communications as a 5th Army / Air Force member: to my Mother, Wanda Lilly (Kirby) Taylor and their daughter Barbara Ellen (Taylor) Junge. I was born, November 26, 1946, Thanksgiving Day around lunchtime in St. Josephs Hospital, Sioux City, Iowa. We lived in a house on Harrison Street in Leeds one block from the Leeds grade school. My Grandmother (Zeta) and Grandfather (Charles) Taylor's house was right next to it, on Central Ave., in Leeds. I started kindergarten when I was four. I remember taking an oral test at the Sioux City School Superintendents Office. I had been asked to draw a girl and boy and I asked the Super, Why ? Didn't he know the difference? I had to tie my shoes myself and count to 10 and recite the alphabet in order to be allowed to start at four instead of waiting another year. I was what they called a "precocious" child. I think Mom and Dad wanted badly to have me in school during the day, while they both worked.

My Mother and Father moved to Minneapolis, Mn. When my kindergarten year was done and school got out for the summer. My Mother got a job in Dayton's clerical department and my Father with Minnegasco, as their head printer. They worked there until they moved to Arnolds Park in the late sixties. My Mother was on the ground floor with setting up structured sales and in on meetings to start the Target chain stores owned by Daytons.

I went to school at Bremer Elementary in N. Minneapolis, and Jordan Junior High 7th and 8tth during which time I loved to sing,(still do) and got to sing a solo in the Minneapolis Auditorium. I got to sing"Winter Wonderland". High school was at Edina Moringside High, I loved sports, was in the choirs and on the Honor Rolls and very much involved in sports and many school plays.

We were living in Edina when I married Tom Ritzer in November of 1963.(Tom never had a chance for he lived on the same street, 7th street, as my four sets of Aunts and Uncles and great Aunts and Uncles and a great grandmother did in Sioux City). We have known of each other for almost our whole lives. When we married, Tom was in the Navy reserves in Sioux City, Ia.. After serving in the Navy Sea Bees as a Plumber and was on the Navy Boxing team. He was also in the Bay of Pigs confrontation over the missiles and helping the Cubans try to gain back democracy. He worked for the Plumbers Union in Sioux City and when we married, we moved to Arnolds Park. Mr. Bill Conner and his wife Ruth lived for the summer here and owned a fixer up house on Iowa street in Arnolds Park. Mr. Conner was Tom's Navy Chief in the reserves and told him they need Plumbers at the Lakes.

So we arrived in December of 1963, and started Tom's Plumbing.I was bookkeeper, orderer and truck unloader, helper and house-keeper and mom of our son, Robert(Rob) Arthur by December of 1964.
Tom became Chief of Police here in the early 70's; besides being a plumber. Tom achieved his Masters Plumbing license in the mid 60's and I got my Journeymen Plumbers License in the late 90's or so.
My Mother and Father moved here from the Twin Cities in late 60's and they both worked at Berkleys in Spirit Lake. They bought the Corner Motel on the corner of Hwy 71 and Linden Dr.(now across from Boonedocks corner). In "68" we traded properties and we ran the Motel as well as did plumbing,
We also worked at and had the first pizza house in Arnolds Park, on our corner; with Al and Mary Foxhoven. We named it,Tom and Al's Pizza Corner.

We had 2 more children Kristina (Tina) Marie and Teresa Lynn. They all went to Arnolds Park School, and still reside in the area. I also took the GED courses to finish at Arnolds Park. Teresa was in the Navy, met her husband there and moved here after she was discharged. They had 2 children...our Grandson, Nicholas and a granddaughter, Cynthia.

We were here when Center Lake only had 2 farm houses close by the lake and pasture was the rest of the land around it.
The same with Moore Lake development area. Very few cottages were in that area and that is what they were, cottages!! No heating, well systems and septic tanks etc. Strictly for summer use on most of them. There was definitely space and land between the cities. There were two drive in theaters in the area and a racetrack in Milford. Pretty much nothing between Milford and Spencer and only a two lane road then.

In the early 80's my parents moved back to the cities (so my Mom could be closer to the University of Minnesota for her cancer treatments) My sister, Barbara, went to work for the Minneapolis Court house. And later went to California for her job at the San Diego County Court House and my father went back to work for Minnegasco. My Mother battled cancer for 13 years before losing the fight in 1983. Tom's Mother and Father, Art and Violet, moved from Sioux City into the house on Iowa street that my parents had moved from. Both my Father and Sister came back to the area permently in late 80's and early 90's. My sister Barbara, found her Husband here, Bill Junge.

Toms brother, Robert (Bob) Ritzer, spent summers here with us and eventually came to the Lakes to work with Tom in the Plumbing field. His wife Cathy came too. Eventually they settled here with their two children Cory and Jeff. They married and made their homes here also with their families.

Tom's sister, Sharon Ritzer, also lived with us for a few years working in Spencer for a time until she married local, Larry Rider. They moved to Arkansas, where Larry worked with Arkansas Fish and wildlife for 25+ years. Their 2 children, Brian and Bobby, still reside in Arkansas as well as Larry and Nancy.

Tom's brother, Larry Ritzer, used to come up From Sioux City and help Tom with Plumbing. He enjoyed it very much. Sometimes his family would come along, his wife Carol, and their two daughters, Rhonda and Rachelle.

Tom's brother, Richard Ritzer also moved here in the 90's to stay with Arthur and Violet and help them with their living needs in old age. His family stayed in Texas, Delores and their two sons, Scott and Steven.

So, our moving to the Lakes brought many relatives here too, even though not all were born here.

When Tom retired from Plumbing, our son Rob bought the business and still owns and operates the Plumbing Shop. Tom went fishing all over and tried to enjoy retirement with the acres outside of Arnolds Park. He also invented a three layer toilet seat. It fit like a regular one on your toilet. One layer for adults, one for small children (no falling thru'), and the lid.

We called it the Ritz Toilet Seat, because of our last name. Sold them all over the country.

Our children all went to school here, and live here and love the area too. Tom and I did buy an area outside of Arnolds Park... and we made and maintained fishing ponds and maintained the grassland and planted corn fields and planted over 150 evergreens and some fruit trees for animal wildlife. Our son, Rob, now has ownership and maintains the area in the same manner. Rob and Grace and Alexis and Kaitlin loved walking the dogs and taking long walks around the ponds and trails.

In the early 90's, I started to become more involved in community activities, The Arnolds Park Centennial for one, and saving Arnolds Park Amusement Park. I became a member of the Arpoki Ladies Club, which has been a constant club since the late 50's. We were a community minded bunch of gals, and helped with community projects and did some on our own also. Just a fantastic group of ladies!

We were all agreed, and in 2018 we made the choice to not have club meetings anymore; due to our ages and people retiring and of course to loss.

I have enjoyed doing some oil painting, I actually have one, in a home in Carmel, Ca.. I like writing poetry and making jewelry, furniture refinishing, catching up on reading, and still helping in the plumbing shop when needed. Tom and I also traveled for a couple years and even spent four winters in "The Valley" in Texas. My favorite places we traveled to were, The Playa Del Carmen in the Yucatan Penninsula, Mexico and to Spain. Then we decided to stay put and enjoy our lakes area family and friends. Due mostly to his health issues, and to be close to the Doctors that he was seeing. Tom lost his health battle and went to be with his Mom and Dad and all Four of his siblings, in January of 2018.

Since Tom's passing, I decided to write a children's book. I had written a poem 20 some years ago for my grandson when his baby sister was born. I read it to both of them when they were little.

It was forgotten for many years. Going through things after Tom's passing; I rediscovered the poem and decided to put it in a book form for children to enjoy. I had met a fantastic painter and decided to ask if she would be interested in illustrating the book. She said yes, and Kassy Abriola, became the Illustrator of our book,"OFF TO DREAMLAND". Which is now in print and ebooks at Amazon, Barnes and Noble and in Libraries and Book Stores.

I still like to travel, be outdoors in the warm sunshine, having plants, and interesting conversations.

I have always enjoyed laughing and feel we should try to look at the lighter sides to most things if at all possible......Laughter is a GOOD MEDICINE.....SMILES ARE CONTAGIOUS. I try to do at least one thing a day to make someone else Smile.

I have a passion about being for the underdog...for them to win... get ahead...or accomplish their goals.
I dislike immensely ...when people say or think... " I can't do it!" or "It can't be done! Especially if they haven't even tried yet. I thoroughly believe, we can all accomplish anything we truly set our minds to, one way or another.....and NEVER, EVER give up on things or people you believe in...Like my Tom, and my children!

That's a condensed version of our lives and my likes and our Lakes Adventure and how we came to LIVE in and LOVE in the Iowa Great Lakes.

Karen Rae (Taylor) Ritzer

Added Note, I have found an old childhood friend from the very early 60's, Dean, is his name, and actually he found me.
He lived up the street from us. We were very good friends. We have rediscovered our friendship. It's like we have never quit conversing, and can talk about anything to someone again. Seems like it's only been a few years between then and now. What a cherished feeling to have a good friend back after almost 60 years. I would recommend rediscovering your old friendships, if at all possible!!

Thank You, Dean.
Karen Rae

In your whole life
you may love
many times
but,
in that whole lifetime
one love will
be held captive
in your heart
and mind
forever!!!

Printed in the United States
by Baker & Taylor Publisher Services